"Dating is more complicated than ever. What Kristin offers in *Beyond the Swipe* is both helpful and hopeful. This is a spiritually practical book for not only dating well but honoring God in the midst of it all. It's full of wisdom, honesty, and vision for how to hold out for and hold on to God's best for you."

Jarrett Stevens
author of *Four Small Words* and pastor of Soul City Church

"I absolutely love Kristin's wit and wisdom in so many areas of life, particularly this topic. She models healthy relationships with others, God, and herself, and her voice is refreshing and encouraging."

Annie F. Downs
best-selling author of *100 Days to Brave* and *Looking for Lovely*

"*Beyond the Swipe* is a must-read for not only those wanting to do dating right but also those of us who have young adults experiencing the dating world. Dating dynamics have certainly changed over the years, and this book has equipped us to help our children. We are so grateful for Kristin's candidness and her ability to delicately balance truth, love, and laughter in these pages. With stakes high and the odds against marriages in today's culture, *Beyond the Swipe* is a timely resource that will breathe much-needed hope, confidence, and knowledge into those seeking long-lasting, self-respecting, and passionate relationships. Thank you, Kristin, for this terrific resource!"

Chris Brown
Ramsey Personality and nationally syndicated radio host, and
Holly Brown
speaker and executive pastor of Embrace Church

"The desire to meet the right person has never changed, but the landscape of how we are finding them definitely has. In this age of smartphones and dating apps, Kristin has written *the* book on how to best navigate this ever-evolving scene. Kristin is both clever and insightful as she offers practical advice. I can't wait to recommend this book to the people around me in the dating world!"

Rodney Anderson
singles director of Buckhead Chur

"*Beyond the Swipe* by Kristin Fry is a helpful book for any of us traversing the tricky and ever-changing waters of dating. Kristin asks good questions, provides sound teaching, and gives us practical tips and tools for navigating our single years with purpose. I found the discussion questions at the end of each chapter challenging and natural to talk about within my group of friends. Read this book and let it be a time of self-reflection. God does not withhold good from us, whatever season of life we are in."

Esther Fleece
speaker and author of *No More Faking Fine*

Honoring God, Respecting Yourself,
and Finding the Right Match

BEYOND
the SWIPE

KRISTIN FRY

Kregel
Publications

Beyond the Swipe: Honoring God, Respecting Yourself, and Finding the Right Match
© 2018 by Kristin Fry

Published by Kregel Publications, a division of Kregel Inc., 2450 Oak Industrial Dr. NE, Grand Rapids, MI 49505.

All photos courtesy of Unsplash.com, from the following artists: *page 13* Brooke Cagle, *page 18* Jamez Picard, *page 39* Guiherme Stecanella, *page 51* Shannon Whittington, *page 58* Azat Satlykov, *page 71* Averie Woodard, *page 87* Caleb Frith, *pages 96 and 125* Priscilla Du Preez, *page 121* freestocks.org, *page 149* Sergey Zolkin, *page 156* Leon Biss.

ISBN 978-0-8254-4513-2

Printed in the United States of America
18 19 20 21 22 23 24 25 26 27 / 5 4 3 2 1

To Jamie,
who believed in me before I believed in myself,
and believed possibility into reality.
Thank you.

Contents

Foreword

Dating . . . Things are a little different these days. When I was growing up, there were two ways a guy would ask a girl out: in person or over the phone. Not a cell phone, a *landline* (remember those?). If someone called the house to speak with me, they needed to make it past whoever answered the phone first—sometimes my dad!

Looking back, I think I'd still choose the old way. It took a bit of courage for the guys to approach us, but it was uncomplicated. I'm thankful for the ones who had the confidence to pick up the phone, call my house, and ask me out. But I'm most thankful for the way my husband, Andy, was clear, kind, and direct with me. He didn't play games. I never had to wonder where our relationship stood. At the appropriate point in the relationship, we talked about it. We had face-to-face conversations.

Fast-forward thirty years. We now have three adult children who have experienced dating in an entirely different context. Every imaginable option is at their fingertips. But that didn't change what we taught them. Honor and respect are timeless. We have taught our sons to respect women, and our daughter to believe she deserves nothing less than that. Most importantly, we wanted them to know that their value and worth have already been established by our heavenly Father.

Andy and I have heard countless stories of what dating looks like these days. I can certainly imagine that it's difficult. But here is what I know to be true: Settling for the wrong person is never the right thing to do. Compromise *does not* end well. And being okay with being treated less than you deserve is selling yourself short. And yet, I've seen so many women do this. I've walked woman after woman through the fallout of heartbreak. This is why I'm so grateful to Kristin for tackling this topic. It's timely and needed because the current of culture is moving so rapidly in the opposite direction.

Through *Beyond the Swipe*, Kristin will empower and equip you to recognize and wait for the guy who will honor and prioritize you. She will help you understand how to successfully navigate today's dating culture and believe that God's best is possible for you. Ladies, you are worth pursuing. If you doubt that, then this book is for you. If you don't doubt that, this book is still for you. You will be given practical steps to take as you move through the dating scene.

I'm so glad you're taking advantage of this opportunity to learn from Kristin. She has been a part of our organization, North Point Ministries, for many years, working with hundreds of single women and men. Kristin is living this story with you, and you will be both challenged and encouraged by her heart and experiences.

Sandra Stanley
Author of *Comparison Trap* and *Breathing Room*

Introduction

We all love happily-ever-after stories. That's why Disney movies and chick flicks are so popular. Despite our past experiences and current realities, and whether we are comfortable admitting it, I believe there is something inside all of us that hopes happily ever after will happen to us too. It's the forever kind of love we want. It's the reason we see Nicholas Sparks movies on opening night. It's the reason we were Team Jacob or Team Edward. It's the reason we throw parties just to watch *The Bachelor* and *The Bachelorette*. And it's the reason there is an entire reality show culture about happily ever after. These series were created to help people find that kind of love too. Unfortunately, the track record of success on such shows is less than ideal. But they keep trying. And I keep watching.

Enter dating apps. You no longer need a reality show to live vicariously through someone else's quest for love. You can access it all on your smartphone. You know where the dating scene is: online. It's the one-stop shop to finding the love of your life. Not only can you find a connection based on geography, common interests, and age requirements, you also get to view a half dozen of their selfies to decide whether you want to swipe right. Well, let's be honest: his profile pic is the deciding factor. Everything else is a bonus. Just kidding. Sort of.

Moment of Truth

I'll stop joking. If you're reading this book, there is a high probability you're on a dating app. Or a few. Or a dozen. You probably have enough stories from your personal experiences to fill your own book. Some are good, some are funny, and some just flat-out make you want to curl into a ball under your covers with a bowl of ice cream. And never come out. Because it can feel hopeless.

If you think I'm about to make an argument for or against dating apps, I'm not. That's not this book. The reason that's not this book is because dating apps are today's normal, and that's not changing anytime soon. It's the way many single people ages eighteen to thirty-nine are dating. In fact, in 2013 there were an estimated twenty-five hundred dating sites in the United States alone, with a thousand more coming online each year betweeen 2014 and 2016.[1] That's a lot. You want to find a truck-driving, country-music listener who lives in the Midwest? There's an app for that. What about a church-going East Coast CEO of a software company by the time he was twenty-four years old kind of guy? Yep. An app for that. Okay, well, maybe not for those specific examples. However, I feel pretty confident they're coming. Then there is Bumble. I mean, it's the Sadie Hawkins dance of dating apps.

All these different dating apps can be exhilarating, exhausting, and confusing—all at the same time—but the truth is that the fabric of culture and our relational lives are interwoven. What do I mean by that? I mean that more often than we care to admit (and by "we" I mean Christians), culture exerts a lot of input into how we interact with each other. Specifically, culture has a lot of influence on how we date.

Now, let me be clear. We still have responsibility. We are responsible for how we respond and how we don't respond. We are responsible for acting and living with integrity, making wise choices, and being kind. But culture can certainly provide the framework for our relationships, and that's exactly what it has done. It has changed the dating scene, and now we have to live in it. That's because technology has changed. What was normal for me in learning to interact with boys as a teenager will never be normal for teenagers today—mainly because they'll never know what a landline is, but that's beside the point. Thanks to mobile devices and location-sensing apps, the whole

world has an opportunity for a date. Smartphones have brought dating to our fingertips. Literally to our fingertips.

So instead of fighting culture, I want to give you hope that you can navigate culture well. In particular, you can be a Christian and navigate dating apps well. You can honor God, respect yourself, and still believe God's best is possible for you in dating. Yes, dating can be hard enough, and dating apps can add a whole new level of confusion to situations where our emotions are already operating on high. Your self-esteem can feel like it's on a roller coaster, leaving you both hopeful and defeated in a matter of swipes. We're going to talk about all of that. And text messaging. Profile pics. Awkward first dates. Being stood up. We're going to talk about how these apps affect the way men interact with us, which has a domino effect on our self-image. We are going to talk about communication, commitment, and boundaries. We're going to talk about God. My hope is to convince you that, in light of all these things, you are worth fighting for. And the right guy will do that.

I'm going to encourage you to believe that you deserve the absolute best in dating and challenge you to settle for nothing less. We are going to talk about how to recognize the man who will honor and respect you. You will be equipped to wait for the man who will make you his priority and to walk away from the man who only treats you as an option. Happily ever after *is* still possible. It just may look different than in the movies.

Even if, at the end of this book, you decide to swear off dating apps until the end of time, I will say, "Good for you." This book can equip you to date well in whatever context. Now granted, the context of this particular book is dating apps, but the principles are universal. And some of you won't swear off dating apps. You will continue to swipe right and left. And I will equally applaud you for it because I'm not trying to get you to delete them from your phone. In fact, I hope you keep them. My goal is to help you.

Disclaimer

I realize that with every new app, there is an increasing number of ways to interact with potential matches. Swiping left and right introduced us to the game, but they're no longer our only options. You can swipe up, swipe down, single tap, double tap, and even shake your phone to backtrack on a regrettable impulse swipe. But wait, there's more. To keep up with our ever-changing technological culture, dating-app companies have decided to jump on the GIF bandwagon. Now GIFs are also an option to express approval for a suggested match.

So, yes, I do realize there are more ways to interact with apps. However, in an already complicated situation, let's just make things simple and use the basic right and left functions. These developers were smart. Left for "no" and right for "yes" are now universal signs in dating. We will all know what I'm talking about.

I should also mention here that I wrote this book with all your friends in mind too. What makes a movie or book even more fun is if you get to talk about it with other people, right? Even though the target audience is women, my bet is that men will also have a lot to say about apps and dating. So grab some girls and guys (if you want)—maybe five or six of each—and talk. Discussions will happen best if you each read the chapter beforehand. I hope you have fun learning from one another.

Hope for the Future

I don't have all the answers, and I can't tell you if you'll get married or who you'll marry. If that's the book you were hoping to read, let me know when you find it, because I'd be interested in reading that book too. But here is what I *can* tell you. There is hope. God cares deeply about you. How you date matters. How men treat you is a big deal, and that should matter to you. And culture doesn't have to be bad.

So if you are interested in reading about those things, let's get started.

Everybody's Doing It

Everyone who's a fan of gymnastics remembers the 2016 Summer Olympics. They generated such widespread media coverage and notoriety it was hard to miss the news coverage, even if you don't like sports.

One event that didn't generate cheering and tear-filled eyes during gold-medal ceremonies, yet attracted plenty of attention: the surge in swipes among athletes during the Rio games. It's unfortunate that at a time when the country's Olympic celebrations should have centered around athletic performances and achievements, the media, instead, hyped the number of "hookups" happening among the athletes. Tinder reported a 129 percent increase in matches in the Olympic Village alone after the first weekend of the games.[2] At the risk of making an unfair assumption, the intent of the majority of those matches likely didn't extend beyond a few hours. That's one unfortunate reality of dating apps.

Yet, dating apps aren't going anywhere. Well, let me rephrase that. Dating apps *are* going somewhere: up. By 2015, the mobile dating industry was generating more than $2.2 billion in annual revenue, with one in ten adults averaging over an hour daily on a dating site or app—numbers expected to continue increasing.[3] Single men and women want to share their lives with someone. It's that simple. The result? We are willing to seize just about any opportunity that will help us find love.

When you think about it, our drive for this forever kind of love isn't that surprising. God created all humans for companionship, to do life with our friends and family (or framily), and ultimately, to do life intimately with just one person. In the Old Testament, Moses penned the following from God: "It is not good for the man to be alone. I will make a helper suitable for him" (Gen. 2:18).

You and I were created by a relational God. In the very beginning, God hardwired us for relational intimacy. Because we were created in the image of God, to be a reflection and representative of God's nature and character, it makes sense that we would also reflect the way he is in relationship with himself, with us, and with the world. Even if you've had past experiences that have clouded your view of marriage, I still believe that somewhere inside of you, you think it's possible to fall in love and stay in love. Forever. And you want it to be possible for you. I believe God designed you like that.

It's no wonder numerous little girls dream of growing up and becoming wives and mothers. Maybe that was you too. Maybe it wasn't. For me, that was never my sole focus. It was *a* dream, but not my *only* dream. I have always been highly ambitious, and I hope my career is the platform where I can best steward my influence. That said, I also have an equal longing to meet a man who will partner with me, and I with him. The point in telling you that is this: wherever you fall on the spectrum of desire for marriage and companionship, it's okay. There is no right and wrong way to view your longing. It's okay, and it's normal.

It's also okay if you're looking into dating apps to find a genuine relationship with the hope of marriage. That's why you're reading this book, right? But before we go any further, there are a few things I want you to know in this chapter. First, you're not alone. Maybe you're embarrassed by the idea of going on Bumble. You may wonder if people will think you're desperate, or if they'll make assumptions about your intentions. If no one else is telling you this, then I want you to hear it from me: there are plenty of people on dating apps who, like you, are trying to live like Jesus and are also looking for forever love. It's also no secret that apps have changed the way people date, in ways that some of the generations before us have never experienced. This is okay too. Dating apps have brought both positive and negative changes to the dating scene. It's important to understand

this if you're going to honor God in your relationships, respect yourself, and know what to look for in a match.

The Reputation of Dating Apps

I believe that the intent behind dating apps is good. What single girl wouldn't want as many options as possible if it will increase her chances of meeting the guy she's going to marry? However, the word *dating* can be applied rather loosely to certain situations.

But it doesn't have to be like that.

I do believe, though, that some of these less-than-ideal reputations of dating apps have caused Christians and non-Christians alike to be hesitant to disclose their use of them. In particular, I've spoken with very few twentysomething single girls who feel comfortable acknowledging they have a dating app on their phone. More specifically, they certainly don't want to confess their current boyfriend is the result of a swipe. At least not initially. One girl who met her boyfriend through an app told me, "After meeting my boyfriend, I was embarrassed when people asked how we met. I always darted around the question. I thought people were going to judge me."

Listen, I get it. People can be overly generous with their judgmental opinions. In turn, this causes us to exercise more caution than normal around topics that feel deeply personal and vulnerable. I've known plenty of girls who've begun a relationship with a guy they've met on an app. And of course, when you're in a new relationship, everyone wants to know, "How did you meet?" That's on the list of top five questions others ask when you start dating someone. More than one girl I've known has answered the question with a straight-up lie. For her, it felt like less of a risk to make up a story than to tell the truth. Because deep down, there is a fear for some women that being on a dating app means you're desperate.

What's Your Story?

I'm guessing you can relate to that fear—or at least know someone who can. I've worked with thousands of young single Christian women over nearly two decades. As a result, I've heard hundreds of stories about dating, relationships, and dating apps. Everyone has a story about how a dating app ended up on their phone. After all, apps just don't appear on smartphones. They are not preloaded when you purchase your phone from the store. You actually have to make a conscious decision to go to the app store, choose what you want, and download it. Maybe it was that time you swore you'd never get on an app—but you did. Or the time you said you'd never go out with anyone you met that way—and you did. For some of you, it was your New Year's resolution to date more. Or to date period.

The contexts are different, but the bottom line is the same: "Dating apps were not for me, but I decided to try it because [fill in the blank]." After all, it's hard to meet new people. You can only change your traffic pattern so many times before you run out of options. Let's face it. Even Waze is only going to give you so many new routes before you have to face reality: you're going to sit in traffic. There is nothing wrong with wanting to meet and date new people in hopes that maybe, just maybe, he will be your *happily ever after.*

So, you go for it. You download the app. You swipe right. So does he. It's been a long time since you were this excited about a first date. Or maybe this is your first date and your stomach is filled with butterflies and nervous anticipation thinking about the what-ifs? The date goes well. You float through your front door on a pillow of clouds. The next day . . . nothing. The day after . . . nothing. And, just like that, you feel more defeated than before you got on the app.

So you open up your phone and start swiping. But this time there is added pressure. Even though you both swipe right, you are now aware that there are still hundreds, if not thousands, of other options—all within a finger's reach. *Maybe I should change my picture, change my interests, or rewrite my profile. Is this really the best photo of me? I look pretty, right? Will someone else think so?* Within seconds, all these thoughts flash through your mind. You rotate a few pictures to the front and keep going. Because deep down, you are hopeful that *happily ever after* might still exist for you. But some days, it feels like it might not. I get it.

Or maybe you were just curious. Your friends were using the apps and they seemed to be having fun. They were meeting guys outside of their normal traffic patterns and friend groups. Dinner conversation among your friends increasingly revolved around whatever guy someone was messaging or going out with. It may have felt like hype to you, but you still wanted to know what it was all about. In fact, I'd bet that you know someone who met their husband through a dating app. And if you were being completely honest, a part of you felt like you might be missing out on something. So you thought, "Why not give this a shot?"

It seemed as though you had met every single guy within a fifty-mile radius. You were seeing the same faces, it was the same scene, and you thought, "Is this all there is?" Or maybe no one was asking you out. Ever. In fact, dating wasn't something you were comfortable with because you'd never done it. It was embarrassing. Family gatherings were all the same: "Are you dating anyone?" No. Still no. Just like the last time you asked. You spent Friday nights (and many Saturdays) on the couch with a chick flick. You prayed, you hoped, and you waited. Nothing. You thought, "God, am I doing something wrong?" As a single person, it can feel like a lot of pressure to try and put yourself out there.

For some of you, you never imagined being single at whatever age you are. Others of you love being single right now and dating is part of the fun. I remember, when I was nine years old, sitting in the bed of my dad's old pickup truck with my best friend. My dad had a camper shell that went over the bed of the truck, with a few shag carpet benches to sit on. It was the eighties; what can I say?

For whatever reason, my best friend and I loved to hang out in his truck on Saturday afternoons. We'd listen to Madonna on cassette tapes on our mini boom box and dream about the future. I distinctly remember saying that I would be married with two kids by the time I was twenty-five. That would give me plenty of time to get one or maybe two degrees and start my perfect career. That's how my nine-year-old brain worked. It never once crossed my mind that life would not work like that. Spoiler alert: it didn't.

I could go on with lists of reasons for downloading dating apps, but you get the point. We are motivated to do things because we have an expectation of a certain result. The same rule applies to how we date and who we date.

It's Not the Same Anymore

However you found yourself on dating apps, with more than twenty-five hundred apps to choose from, dating can still be challenging. As a culture we're constantly learning how dating apps are changing the way we date. Ironically, in attempting to simplify our world through technology, we've unintentionally added new layers of complication. For example, most of us have had the experience of meeting a guy we were not initially attracted to, but as we got to know him, he became incredibly attractive. Likewise, a lot of us have had the opposite experience. When you decide to take your dating life online, getting to know someone first feels like a luxury of the past that is no longer afforded to you. Instead, you get one profile pic to communicate everything you want to communicate about yourself. Choose wisely.

To make complicated matters worse, everything on the internet seems to live forever, including my Turkey Trot race time from 1998. When you create your online dating profile, you're also making a decision to allow your personal life to be permanently searchable for the rest of recorded human history. If you are hearing that idea for the first time, let me repeat myself: dating online means you are now publicly and forever documenting your private life. Be careful. (Ah, the things we do for love.)

I've spoken with many married men and women about dating apps. They typically listen with wide eyes and open mouths, since they have a hard time wrapping their heads around our style of dating. This is real, folks. Welcome to our world. But here's the good news: dating app stories are some of the funniest stories out there. With just one good dating tale, you can have an entire room in stitches. But when sides stop aching and the jokes wind down, a common response goes something like this: "I am so glad I don't have to deal with that." An even more interesting, yet equally common, response is: "Had I been given the option of hand-selecting all of the qualities I was looking for in my future spouse, I would not have ended up with the person I did." That's when the single people get wide-eyed.

Before dating apps, there was no option to prescreen your potential match for your most ideal qualities in a mate. This essentially means you're looking for a match based on unrealistic perfection. But technology never disappoints, so now we have that option. Insert the high-ten emoji. (Which Christians like to call the "praise hands." But nope, I'm still arguing for the high ten. Look it up.) The point is, as women, we know that we've only been matched with the men who are interested in the qualities we've listed.

In addition, as men are scrolling through their phones, our picture needs to be attractive enough to cause them to pause long enough to swipe right. There is no opportunity for the subtle glance or smile from across the room. The only opportunity is a quick decision on a screen. Women most certainly feel the pressure of this. Plus, we know that everyone to some degree is going to misrepresent themselves. I mean, really, are you actually planning on posting a picture of your "bad side" with "that face" in "that outfit"? It's doubtful. On the flip side, women are also forced to make a snap judgment based on a picture and highly edited information.

Dating apps have also opened up a whole new strategy to dating. There is a strategy to choosing your profile pics, your complementing pictures, writing your profile, choosing your interests . . . and don't get me started about the initial messaging. (We'll talk about all these in coming chapters.) I know a few people who change their location radius to one mile or less when they go to church on Sundays. This increases their chances of being matched with someone who attends the same church. When my senior pastor and employer, Andy Stanley, first learned about strategies in dating, his response was, "When I was growing up, it never dawned on me that I needed one of those. There's a strategy? In *dating*?"[4] Oh yes, Andy, yes. There most certainly is a strategy. That is the gift dating apps have given us.

Change Can Be Good

Dating apps have definitely changed the game. There is no question about that. For many, the changes have been helpful, but not without cost. The most common benefit of dating apps, as said by single girls who use them, is that they have taken the pressure off. One girl told me, "It's not that I had an overly serious view of dating to begin with, but I definitely have a more casual view of it now. Before, I felt a lot of pressure on dates. I think I'm now a little more willing to go out with people just to get to know someone different, even if I don't initially think I'm compatible with them."

The attention you get when you're on the app also feels good. A lot of girls are not getting attention from men in their day-to-day lives, and they want it. I'm not talking about the unhealthy, I-can't-live-without-it kind of attention. I'm talking about the normal, everyday compliments. (I will address in a future chapter how to recognize when your desire for attention goes bad.) But it does numbers for your self-esteem when you swipe right on an attractive guy and he swipes right too. Most girls struggle with feeling attractive. This looks different for everyone, but I've yet to meet a single girl who has not, at some point in her life, wondered if someone would find her beautiful. Particularly for the girl who is new to the dating scene, it's a confidence booster when you open the app to find three connections waiting for you. Actually, it's a confidence booster for anyone. Every girl needs to be reminded she is pretty. Every girl deserves that. Every girl. That can certainly be a benefit of dating apps.

Here's another thing I like about dating apps. Because apps have encouraged a more casual approach to dating, this allows girls who never would have been asked out the opportunity to practice interacting with the opposite sex. For example, I have a friend who ended a multiple-year relationship and realized she didn't know how to date. She decided to simultaneously download two separate dating apps for the sole purpose of learning how to date again. She wanted to feel comfortable having conversations with strangers, and being open to new people. She was also looking for an outlet to practice basic conversational skills within personal boundaries. I don't know about you, but to me this is a great idea. I appreciate the fact that dating apps give you the opportunity to practice healthy relational skills. If you need permission to *practice* dating, consider this permission granted.

 Dating apps give you the opportunity to practice healthy relational skills.

I know of a girl who genuinely loves dating and dating apps. She doesn't take herself or the dates too seriously. In fact, she has regularly gone on a Tinder date on her way to a Tinder date. If it's a Saturday, she will oftentimes schedule breakfast, lunch, and dinner dates—with three different guys. To me, that sounds painfully exhausting, but more power to her. She's having fun, and there is nothing wrong with that. For her, it's a way to spend time with people she may not otherwise have the chance to meet. It's also worth it to squeeze as many dates in as possible to ensure that happens.

Rejection Is Still Rejection

The unfortunate reality is that while there may be thousands of apps to give you hope that your *forever love* is out there, there is equal opportunity for those same apps to tell you that he's not. As good as it feels when an attractive guy swipes right, it feels just as bad—if not worse—when he doesn't. I know plenty of girls who have deleted apps from their phones because the virtual rejection was getting to be too much. Then months would go by and the everyday scene proved equally depressing, and the apps returned. It's a vicious cycle.

Piled on top of that is the rejection after a few dates. For a girl, there is a reason the rejection feels so heavy. When a guy rejects us, it's not just an immediate death of the relationship (or potential relationship), it also feels like the death of a dream. Even though the only thing ending is that relationship, in our emotion-laden hearts and minds, it feels as though all hope has been lost for finding someone to spend forever with. Remember, God has designed us for a forever kind of love, so it's normal that we desire it. Regardless of what our past and current experiences have or have not taught us, that kind of love is *in* us.

If you have ever watched an exit interview from *The Bachelor,* it's the reason that nine times out of ten the ones who've been rejected say something along the lines of, "I knew I wasn't lovable. No good thing ever happens to me. No one ever chooses me." And, wait for it: "What's wrong with me?" To the viewer, the reaction never quite seems to match the circumstance. But to the girl, I believe it's her subconscious attempt at trying to sort through the pain she's feeling. Let's face it, ladies, our irrational thoughts feel perfectly rational when our hearts have been broken.

Still, I always have some key questions running through my mind when I watch those interviews, starting with: "Are you listening to yourself?" C'mon, girls, this is only a no for that one person, not a no to your forever. Have you forgotten that there are still seven billion other people in the world? I don't know about you, but to me, that's a lot of people—and a lot of opportunity for a great match. Besides, don't these contestants know most of those people are on dating apps? They should try it. But, whatever, you're right, no one will ever want you.

Girls believe that rejection extends far beyond the end of that one relationship. When rejection comes, even in the form of a left swipe, it's not always easy to see that another great guy will come along. But, I get it. When it's your life, it's hard to see clearly. I've done it too. The fact is, getting rejected on an app still hurts like getting rejected face-to-face. The difference is apps have merely given us more ways to face rejection.

Another negative side effect of dating apps is poor interactions between men and women. When I say poor, here is what I mean. Because there are so many options available to men through an app, women can be reduced to a number—or an object—instead of a person. You may go out with a guy and have a great time because the connection is real and obvious. You both feel it. But instead of him calling (or texting) you for another date, he wants to give a few more girls a try first, before he makes any decisions about his second date. One girl told me, "Because the norm is around texting and not calling, making last-minute plans instead of planning ahead, it's changed the definition of dating for me. When I go out with a guy, I know that I'm potentially just one of two or three girls that he is going out with that week. Instead of feeling special, I'm just his next date."

If you wanted to be reduced to a number, you would have signed up for *The Bachelor*. As a girl, that doesn't feel good. When women are reduced to a number time and time again, matches become less and less meaningful. And when women become just a number, they feel devalued and less respected. But dating is not supposed to be like that. Relationships are not supposed to be like that.

There's an interesting thing that's happening though: women are feeling the effect of this. You may be one of them. Some of you are sharing these sentiments and struggles within your friend circles, but most of you are not going around making public statements about your feelings. Instead, you continue the cycle, keeping your thoughts to yourself but feeling like there is no other alternative.

The problem is that when *some* people participate in poor dating, it impacts everybody's prospects and experience. Not everyone has to be dating well, only a critical mass. Women, we must strive to become the critical mass to make a positive change. I am confident that it's possible. Just as one critical mass can ruin it for the rest of us, we are going to be the critical mass that makes it better. Right now. Us.

That's why I don't want you to give up. I know dating is hard, and sometimes it can feel like all hope is lost. But there is also more opportunity for things to go really, really well. With that comes hope, and hope trumps all. My encouragement to you is to not lose heart. Trust me, I know it can be hard. I know what it's like to face rejection from left swipes, from guys I've only dated for a few weeks, and from a guy that I gave years of my life to. All of it hurts just the same.

 Letting go of one thing allows you to make room for something better.

However, what I have found to be true in my own life is that letting go of one thing allows you to make room for something better. Remember what I said earlier about God creating us as relational beings? The God who knows you best knows the future. Even when you can't see what he's doing, he is at work. So, trust that God has not forgotten about you and move forward with confidence.

Questions for Reflection

1. Have you ever lost hope or been tempted to give up on dating? Why?
2. What is the reputation of dating apps among your friends and in your social circles? Has that reputation affected your use of dating apps?
3. Assuming you use dating apps, have you developed a personal strategy? What have been the results so far? Are there ways you need to adjust your strategy to get different results?
4. In what ways might you need to change the way you interact with men through dating apps, via texting, and in person? If you are happy with your interactions, as you read through this book, think through ways you can encourage or challenge other women in their interactions with men.

He Already Swiped Right

Every year, Dictionary.com announces its word for the year, based on data from word searches on their website. In 2015, the winner was "identity."[5] The reason I remember it so clearly is because I was so shocked. Of all the words in the human vocabulary, people had used the internet to search for the definition of "identity" over any other word! Didn't they already know it? I suppose I had taken for granted that we all have a basic understanding of who we are—and who we are not. But 2015 was the year questions about marriage and gender burst into the forefront of politics, news, and social media. At the core of the search, I believe that people still wanted to know things like: *Who am I? How do I know? Who defines me?* These are significant questions that go to the core of who we are.

I have discovered that, culturally, numerous categories inform our identity. Family, friends, relationships, what you do (or don't do) for work, personal perceptions, and past experiences. Now, you may be thinking, "I thought this was a book about dating." It is. However, if you don't have a firm grasp on your personal identity, it will be easy to fall into the trap of allowing external ideas, circumstances, or people to define you. In particular, I want to prevent you from allowing the person you're dating or that relationship to dictate your identity. Because the truth is that all the previously mentioned things are fluid. They can come and go at any time—the living, breathing definition of "impermanent." If you allow those things to define yourself, then what? What happens when they're gone? Who are you then?

Before we get too far into talking about who we are going to date and how we are going to go about dating, we need to talk about who's doing the dating. And that *who* is you. We'll start here. It's important. You may not believe that, but I'm hoping to convince you otherwise by chapter's end. Maybe what you believe about yourself isn't something you've put much thought into—at least, not with any concentrated, intentional effort. Then again, you could be the contemplative and self-reflective type, finding great joy in dissecting your internal mental world. That's me, by the way. When I get carried away, processing and evaluating my internal belief system turns into a part-time job. Sometimes I think I really need to get out more. Maybe a few of you can relate.

Wherever you fall on the awareness scale about your identity and personal belief system, it's important to take it one step further. The reason is simple. My goal is to convince you that what you believe about yourself, and who you believe you are, affects every aspect of your life. This not only has implications for your self-esteem, but also affects how you interact with other people and how you allow them to interact with you. What you believe about yourself affects your interactions with those you date and how you go about dating them. Your beliefs determine your behavior, and it can all be boiled down to one simple question: "Who am I?"

 What you believe about yourself affects your interactions with those you date.

Did you know that most of your twentysomething years are spent trying to figure out who you are? That's not a bad thing. In fact, it's perfectly normal. If you fall into that age bracket, breathe deep. You're normal. Give yourself permission to not have all the answers yet. If you find yourself outside of that age bracket, that's okay too. Hopefully, this chapter will provide a framework for giving you some of the answers you didn't know you were looking for.

The reality, however, is that too many people will spend their entire lives trying to figure this out. And they never will. I'm going to argue that there is a fundamental answer to this question, "Who am I?" that, answered now, will save you a lot of tension and confusion in the end.

Our Brains and the Internet

"Who am I?" can be a hard question to ask. First, because it's deeply personal. And second, because when we do ask it, we don't always feel satisfied with the answers we uncover. As human beings, we don't like feeling less than confident about a question that feels so important. So we keep searching for different answers.

This is part of why we love Google. Can I get an amen? The World Wide Web is a wealth of information. It's a host for really anything you could want to know about—well, almost anything. I wondered what the internet would tell me about my identity, so I typed in, "Who am I?" in the search bar. Certainly, I'm not the only person who has asked the question, and I know I'm not the first person who has gone to the internet for answers. As I suspected, the internet did not let me down.

In my search feed, I found pages and pages of tests and quizzes to measure my personality, skills, and talents, all in an attempt to help me discover who I am. Don't get me wrong. I love a good personality assessment. I think they are great tools for both personal and professional use. However, they are just that. Tools. They give you a sense of what you're good at, what your personality is like, or how you respond in stressful situations. But I still don't believe this satisfies the core of the question: "Who am I?"

Here's a little psychology for you; just hang with me. Did you know that our brains are working 100 percent of the time to find answers to the questions we ask ourselves?[6] It's fascinating, really. But this also means that when we wonder about identity questions, our brain wants an answer to that question too. We were created with minds that want to make sense of the world. What's even more interesting is that when there is not a concrete answer, our brain has been programmed to make stuff up. (How crazy is that?) The reason: our brains are incapable of living without answers. Instead of not having an answer, it will make something up and then convince you that it's true.

Let me give you an example. Someone invites you to a get-together at their house. There will be lots of people there you've never met. You think to yourself that you should go. It's a great opportunity to meet new people. You spend sixty minutes too long picking out your outfit because, after all, you've never met these people and no need to make a bad first impression. But this lends itself to arriving thirty minutes late. This works in your favor though, since no one wants to be the first to arrive. Besides, it's always easier to walk into a crowded room as opposed to an empty room when you know very few people there. It allows you to blend in if need be and ease some of the anxiety of wondering if people are going to stare at you for coming in alone. Don't pretend I'm the only one who has ever thought about this.

You get out of your car and walk in. There are lots of people already in the house, you don't see anyone you recognize, and you haven't spotted your friend who extended the invite. You stand near the entryway for what feels like an eternity. No one has walked up to you or smiled in your direction. Not that you need a babysitter, but a simple acknowledgment would ease the tension that's now building inside. In as soon as the first ten seconds of your arrival, here are all the thoughts that can go through your mind: (1) No one is talking to me. They must not like me. (2) I can't see my friend. What if she left and now I'm here alone? (3) I knew I should have worn something else. Why did I think it was a good idea to have my hair like this? (4) Why didn't I bring someone with me? (5) That's it, this is a bad idea, I should not have come. So, you leave.

In a mere ten seconds, your brain has not only tried to make sense of a new environment, but given you an interpretation. Consequently, you start believing things that are not even true. And then you act on them. That's just how our brains are programmed.

Now why am I telling you all of this, and what does it have to do with dating? The same rules apply to what we believe about ourselves. If we can't confidently answer the question, *Who am I?* our brains will lie to us and make stuff up—because they can't handle not having an answer. The interesting thing is that we don't always know we're doing this. Instead, we subconsciously find ourselves acting out of something that we believe and don't even know why we believe it. With the party example, the thought never crossed your mind that any or all those things may not be true. It didn't matter; you believed it, and acted.

In some ways, it's really cool that we are hardwired to have answers to questions. For example, this can be helpful when we walk into job interviews. Truthfully, we may not know if we can do the job, but our brains fill the gaps with all the reasons we are qualified, so we apply! But the downfall is that if we don't have actual facts to work with, there is a danger that we could believe something false about ourselves *without even realizing it*. And when we believe false things about ourselves, this can cause us to act in ways that are counter to God's best for us when it comes to relationships.

Who Am I?

I don't know what it was like for you growing up, but I tried to answer the question, *Who am I?* in several different ways. For years, I believed and acted from a number of false assumptions. I come from a broken home where my parents were divorced while I was in middle school—as if middle school years weren't complicated enough. While my parents were trying to salvage their lives, I was trying to fend for mine.

In ways I didn't realize, this created an inner identity deficit and set a pattern in motion for the next fifteen years. This pattern created a neediness to seek out friends, relationships, and accomplishments to affirm my sense of worth. It's not that friends or achievements are bad, but they became my entire identity. In my younger years, if I had a fight with friends, I felt devastated. I would write them these passive-aggressive letters detailing all the ways I was the victim in the scenario, and then put them in the mail (because email and cell phones were not yet a thing). I tried to lay every guilt trip imaginable on the offender. Because I needed this friendship, I was lost without it. I didn't know who I was.

In college, my identity revolved around grades. In high school, I could extend very little effort and still get all As, but in college I had to really work. I learned that going to class actually mattered. And I did not get all As. Not even close. So, I felt like such a failure. I was embarrassed, and even though no one knew my grades, I still imagined that everyone thought I was stupid. Not surprisingly, I started to define myself as stupid. I did what I needed to do just to get by. I remember standing in line on graduation day thinking to myself, "I hope I did enough to pass."

Thankfully, I did pass and went on to grad school, which felt like a clean slate. School was easy because I loved it, and I felt smart again. But when I graduated I didn't get the dream job I had envisioned. Everyone else seemed to get theirs, but not me. Here I was with a master's degree and no one would hire me. (I could have gone to Starbucks or Target for a job, but I wasn't interested in that. Therefore, "no one" would hire me.) I did contract work for different organizations, worked as a substitute teacher for a few years and at some summer camps and all the yearly sales at Nordstrom. (I am now confident you get an extra special reward in heaven if you work retail.) Still, I felt like a failure. Like something was wrong with me.

My entire identity was wrapped up in all these external things. Apart from relationships and achievements, I had no idea who I was. More importantly, I thought that who I was was not enough. For me, this led to a downward spiral of emotions. My job wasn't able to affirm who I was. I wasn't dating anyone at the time, so I couldn't rely on a guy to "prove" that I was worth knowing and loving. I couldn't find anything external to confirm that I was worth something, so I began to wonder if God was playing a joke on me. "Is this really my life? Am I really not worth anything?" Let me tell you, it was a dangerous, slippery slope to stand on. One negative doubt led to another doubt until I was wondering what I was even doing here at all. I felt like wasted space.

Now, your life probably looks different from mine. Some of you might answer the question, *Who am I?* with the name of the guy you're dating. You are the person who is always in a relationship. In fact, you don't know the last time you weren't. Quite frankly, you are not all that interested in finding out. You are secure in who you are—when you are dating someone. As soon as that relationship ends, though, you feel completely lost. And when you find yourself in this situation, you get involved with the next guy who comes along. He may not be great, but at least you're not alone. You compromise. You settle for less than you deserve—and probably much less than what you even want. All in an attempt to fill the void and find security and self-worth.

Maybe your identity is in your job. Having the right one, or getting the right one. You need the job that culture defines as good and important, or the job that your parents chose for you. And when you have that job, you will be enough, complete, and confident. But what if you're not?

Maybe you get so wrapped up in the social media world that you wonder how five minutes just turned into forty-five. It's a comparison game. Now, this is one we all can relate to: comparing ourselves to someone else's highlight reel. Why don't we look that good, have that hair, those clothes, that boyfriend? *What's wrong with me?*

Or, are you the one doing the posting? Your sense of self-worth and confidence rises and falls on the attention you get from pictures and posts—or lack thereof. But what's even worse is how bad you feel about yourself when you see a picture on social media of your friends out somewhere, and you weren't invited. You're crushed.

The reason it matters how you define yourself—and why it's important to sort this out apart from dating—is because what God says about you is what's most true about you. It took me far longer than I'd care to admit to understand this. While I knew the truths of what God said about me in my college years, I didn't live *like they were true* when I graduated. Maybe you don't know what God says about you. I'd start there. But even then, in my life, it took not just knowing what God says about me in the Bible. I also needed a group of trusted friends who could reflect back to me when my behaviors didn't line up with what I knew to be true. This required being honest with myself and with them. Over time, I stopped looking to people, things, my reputation, achievements, relationships, and jobs to fill my sense of identity. None of that is most true about me—or you. None of it. Instead, I could enjoy all those things for what they were, without expecting something in return. My life was awesome with them but also didn't fall apart without them. However, getting to that point didn't happen overnight. It was a process for me. And it will be for you too.

 If you base your identity on things that can constantly change, then you will have an identity that is constantly changing.

At the risk of sounding like a broken record, what you believe determines how you behave. What you believe affects how you live and interact with men, even on dating apps. Indeed, well beyond dating apps. If what you believe about who you are is coming from other people's opinions or false messages you've picked up along the way, you will act and behave accordingly. If you don't have confidence that you are of great worth—that you are beautiful and desirable just as you are—then you'll be tempted to get into situations with men that you later regret. You may find yourself in bed with a guy, because you thought maybe then he'd love you. Maybe he did (or you convinced yourself that he did) for that one night. Or maybe you find it hard to genuinely be there for other women because they feel like a threat to you. Instead, you pick them apart behind their backs, lie to their faces, and use social media to prove to yourself that you're better than them. And maybe that does make you feel better about yourself—for the next thirty minutes. But if you base your identity on things that can constantly change, then you will have an identity that is constantly changing. And your life will become like a hamster wheel, always searching but feeling like you keep ending up back at the beginning.

Who God Says You Are

Thankfully, God has a lot to say about identity. God has a lot to say about you. Paul, an author of numerous books in the New Testament, wrote a letter to a group of people called the Ephesians. He was writing them to remind them of the things that God had said about their identity. In some of the opening lines of the letter, we read this: "For he [God] chose us in him before the creation of the world to be holy and blameless in his sight. In love he predestined us for adoption to sonship through Jesus Christ, in accordance with his pleasure and will" (Eph. 1:4–5).

At first pass, those two lines may sound confusing, but don't let that be a distraction. If you hang with me, I promise that those two sentences will reveal something about you that you may never have known before. In context, Paul is reminding the Ephesians of the gospel of Christ, and telling them how they fit into that gospel. In essence, in these two specific verses, Paul is saying *this* is who you are. Our identity all hangs on one word: adopted. If you've been a church person for any length of time, there is a chance you've heard someone liken this verse to adoption in our present age. In the way that adoptive parents choose a child to be a part of their family, God chooses us to be in his family. There is truth to that, for sure, but that analogy barely scratches the surface of what Paul is communicating about our identity.

At the time Paul wrote this letter, the Roman culture surrounding the Ephesians believed a worldview that your body had to be perfect; I suppose it's not all that different than the messages we hear today. But this worldview was so extreme that if a baby was born with any sort of disfiguration, however slight, the birth parents had governmental permission to take their newborn outside the city limits and discard it.[7] To be blunt, they could throw away their baby for being born imperfect. Can you imagine? This was a very common practice and no one ever thought twice about it. These sweet babies were piled on a nearby hill merely because someone deemed them defective.

Here is where it gets even crazier. People in the town knew where these infants were being discarded; it was common knowledge. They would go up there, pick through the babies, and find ones to either fill their brothels or to use as slaves. The reasoning? It was much cheaper to raise an infant than buy a slave.

But the story isn't done. If you were rich and childless, you could adopt a slave to be your son. Remember who the slaves are? The imperfect babies all grown up. *Adoption*, in its literal sense, means "son placing." So these fathers would take the sons (the imperfect sons), the sons would accept, and they'd be placed in their new family. Naturally, the slave would have had debts, but once adopted, those debts were canceled. It was just how the system was set up.

The slave, now an adopted son, received a new name and a new identity as part of this new family. And it was irrevocable—you could not un-adopt a child. But this is the most bizarre part of the whole thing: It wasn't just rich, childless families who would adopt. If there were fathers who didn't like their sons, they too were allowed to disown their biological child and adopt a slave instead. Let me be very clear. The Romans could disown natural children but they could not, under any circumstances, disown adopted children.

Does it now make more sense why this word *adopted* was so powerful in Paul's letter? The people who were reading it would have been blown away that Paul would even choose such a word to describe them. The only frame of reference was that the adopted ones were the imperfect ones, and they lived in a world that said being perfect was the only way to survive. But these words from Paul stated that God declared them perfect, just as they are. That God took the meaning of the word *adoption* and spun it on its head. Out of God's great love, he chose them, adopted them, and invited them into their new identity—Christ's identity. God chose them exactly as they were. God, the Father, went after *them* specifically. This idea was the exact opposite of their worldview. And yet, it's true. Just as it's also true for you and me.

God redefined adoption and gave it a new meaning. He tells you that you're chosen, you're perfect, you cannot be disowned, and

Before
you ever got on a
dating app, God
swiped right.
On you.

your identity cannot be altered. Ever. Everyone in town knew that the infants would be thrown out. Instead, Paul gives us a picture of a God who went past the city limits, up the hill, scooped up those who had been discarded, and declared them as his. He gave them a solid, secure, permanent identity—one that could never be altered by external circumstances, people, or things.

That, my friends, is what God did for you. To put it in today's terminology, God already swiped right on you. Before you ever got on a dating app, God swiped right. On you. You only need to accept and believe that for yourself.

I am not saying that relationships, jobs, and accomplishments are not important. Those are great things. Important things. Fun things. If you were to continue reading on your own in Ephesians, you would see that Paul talks about God having a plan for your life, but it first involves you believing what's most true about you and being confident in your identity as God defined it. If you don't get your identity right first, it's easy for the rest of life to get out of whack.

It's really common for us women to believe that we are either not good enough or unlovable, most likely stemming from a past negative experience. We believe what other people think about us, say to us, or do to us instead of turning to what God thinks about us, says to us, and has done for us. When we begin to believe lies about ourselves, they inform our identity without us even realizing it. The outcome is that we start doing crazy things, particularly in regard to men and relationships, subconsciously trying to fill in the gaps about who we think we are. We start dating men we shouldn't and hanging on to relationships past their expiration date. We say yes to things we aren't really that interested in because we've told ourselves we won't get any better, or we don't deserve any better. We convince ourselves that's all we are worth. The good news is that God chose us based on nothing we did or earned. We didn't have to perform our way into his family. Which is even better news, since that also means we'll never be able to perform our way out of his family.

God says your identity is not up for debate. The case has been closed. You have been chosen and you are loved. Therefore, your identity is secure. End of story. Let's give our brains these facts to work with so they don't need to look elsewhere to fill in the missing pieces. No more Google searches.

Truth in Real Life

Now what? Knowing what you believe, why you believe it, and then living accordingly matters. But you may be thinking, "Okay, I get it. But how do I live like that?" In my experience, here are three things that have been most helpful to me in living with confidence in who God says I am:

1. *Know what God says about you.* God has given us an entire Bible full of truths about himself and us. If you haven't developed a habit of reading it, it's never too late to start. Knowing who God says you are is a great weapon against the lies that come at us about our identity and worth.

2. *Believe what God says about you and act like it.* It's one thing to know what God says, but it's another thing to believe it and allow it to change how you live. I remember when I was learning how to wakeboard. I jumped in the water and someone yelled to me, "Kristin, you're an athlete! You can do this!" I was incredibly hesitant about my ability to learn something new, but that comment changed everything. Even though I had no clue what I was doing and was deathly afraid of the water, that comment gave me confidence and caused me to believe that I *could* learn this new sport. And I did! The same principle applies to what God says about us. If we let it, it will change the way we live.

3. *Surround yourself with people who know and believe what God says.* There will always be times when we doubt ourselves and doubt what God says about us. That's normal; it's called being human. But these are also the times when our friends can fill the gaps and speak over us the truth that we are having a hard time believing. There have been plenty of times when my friends have stepped into my

life and believed in me when I was having a hard time believing in myself.

Confidence

Who are you? You are deeply loved, chosen, and secure. What you believe about yourself determines how you behave. When you accept this for yourself, it will free you up to do just about anything else, with no strings attached. Your identity is not dependent on external situations or people. It can't be taken away, added to, or subtracted from. Awareness of this will give you confidence. Confidence in life, and confidence in dating.

You will have confidence to say no to men when you need to and to say yes to them when you want to. These men don't define you and neither does a relationship with them. This gives you the confidence to expect only the best for yourself and to know that you deserve only that.

What's most true about you is what God says about you. When you keep your eyes on God, you'll be surprised what you start to look like. When you believe that you are someone worth dying for, that changes everything. When you know what you're worth, you will know what to expect. And the right men will be attracted to that.

Let the dating begin!

Questions for Reflection

1. What does it mean to you personally that God already swiped right on you?
2. Pretend someone asked, "Who are you?" What would you say? Do you believe it? Do you act like it's true?
3. Have you ever dated someone you didn't really want to date? Why?
4. What is one thing you can do this week to help you live in light of God's truth about you?

What Are You Looking For?

Whether you realize it or not, you've been ordering your days around predecisions your entire life. It's these same predecisions that have informed the conscious decisions you've been making thereafter.

What do I mean by *predecisions*? Let me give you an example. Some of you made a predecision during your junior or senior year in high school that you wanted a career as a software engineer. That decision provided the framework for which colleges you were going to apply to. Once admitted, the thought never crossed your mind to declare early childhood education as your major. Why? Because that's a degree better suited for those who have an interest in children or in teaching. The same rule applied when it came time to apply for jobs: your predecision narrowed down the businesses and organizations to which you applied.

As a side note, some of you are in your late twenties and older and have no idea what you want to be when you grow up. Just by reading the previous sentences, you feel the level of anxiety rising. Take a deep breath. It's okay. However, I'd suggest narrowing your career focus to a few options and taking steps that will eventually lead to a decision. Because the example above still applies.

You also order your daily life around several intentional and subconscious predecisions that have predetermined what you will or will not do each day. You may be someone with a predecision of running a marathon six months from now. Consequently, it's easy to decide to not order dessert after dinner, to go to bed earlier because of a long run the following day, and to drink water instead of soda. (Unless it's Dr. Pepper. I have to be honest: I will always choose Dr. Pepper.) When I've decided to eat healthier before heading to a restaurant, I'm not agonizing over ordering brussels sprouts or French fries. Clearly French fries are not the option of choice. Well, actually, they are the option of *choice*, but certainly not the healthier choice. However, I have managed to convince myself that sweet potatoes fries are equally healthy. Please, if I'm wrong, don't tell me.

This concept applies to every area of life, even when we are unaware of it. When my goal is to grow in my relationship with God, it's natural to organize my days or weeks around spending time with God by reading my Bible and praying, going to a weekend church service, and plugging in a few podcasts on my commute to work every now and then. I'm not waking up each day wondering how I'll spend my time. As a side note, there are plenty of times a few extra hours of sleep have won out over my predecisions, lest you think I'm someone that I'm not. But, my predecisions eliminate some of the other decision-making in the moment and inform how I spend, not all, but good portions of my days.

It's interesting how we can make conscious decisions about less consequential things, but when it comes to dating and relationships, we tend to respond in the moment. We agonize over noncritical decisions like buying the yellow or blue top, or which restaurant to go to for dinner. In many cases of dating, however, we often don't even recognize that it's a decision; we just react. You may open your app and see the notification that you've been matched with not one but two very attractive guys. Score! Who wouldn't be excited about that? They're both cute. Impulses springing into action, it never even crosses your mind that you should consider something else outside of what you're seeing on your screen. In the moment, your next move feels like a no-brainer. Swipe right, double tap, or send them a message. Basically, whatever you need to do to communicate acceptance. Yet, consider that the people we date will eventually lead to the last person we date, which will lead to one of the most important decisions of our lives.

Boiled down to you, will you say, "I do"? Which then begs the question: Is reacting without forethought the best decision I can make?

Before we even get to the (normal) emotional excitement of a match, it's worth deciding what we want in a match. Let's face it, we've all had our share of disappointing matches to the point of being tempted to poke ourselves in the eyes if we get just one more letdown. It's no wonder we want to immediately act when a good one comes through, or at least a "normal" one. (You know what I mean.) Instead, let's think about what we want from a match, or a date, or a significant other. This means being honest with ourselves and giving a long, hard look at what motivates us. We need to ask ourselves whether our feelings and desires really line up with who we want to be, and who we want to be *with*. If we want healthy, exciting, God-honoring dates and relationships, we need to know what we're looking for and what we expect of ourselves—before we're already in the moment.

Motivations

We make choices all the time based on our motivations, as in the example of fries versus brussels sprouts. Dating is no different. When you downloaded the dating app to your phone, there was at least one motivation for doing so. Perhaps you were curious about what your friends were talking about. Or you wanted to know if there were other datable men out there you hadn't already met. Knowing your motivation for dating can be one of the best ways to take charge of your own dating app experience.

One girl in her late twenties I spoke with had never been on a date. I assured her there are plenty of women who can relate with her life experience (or lack thereof) but feel embarrassed to admit it. As a side note, when no one with the same experience openly talks about it, this creates a perception that you must be the *only* one who is such-and-such age who has never been on a date. In fact, that's just not true. However, this girl decided she wanted to do something about her lack of dating experience and downloaded a few dating apps. I applauded her bravery. Subsequently, she was matched with some ideal and not-so-ideal guys, as you can imagine, but she has now had several first dates. That is the part I really like about dating apps. They are a great tool for providing opportunities to normalize going through life as a twentysomething (or any age) woman. As this girl defined normal, it meant going on dates with single men. She knew what her motive was: to go on a date. Mission accomplished.

But there are other motivations for using dating apps as well. Recently the dating app, Hinge, conducted a survey to see what motivated people to use their platform, and based on the feedback they decided to do a redesign and rebrand.[8] The feedback? Among other things, they found that 90 percent of legacy Hinge users swipe on swiping apps when they are bored, and 30 percent go on dates assuming they won't work out.[9] As much as I wanted to be shocked by these findings, I wasn't. My guess is that some of you aren't shocked either.

Still, I was disappointed. I do realize there are some people whose only motivation is to pass time and have some fun, so they treat dating apps like a game: How many mutual swipe rights can they get in one night? Others make it out to be a competition. I'm certain this would break a myriad of privacy laws, but I'd be curious to see data on the times of day that people swipe on their apps. My guess is that a high percentage takes place after ten or eleven at night. This is unfortunate for those of us who are on dating apps with good and hopeful intentions of meeting a great guy.

In light of the data, Hinge made some adjustments to their app. They changed the way you define yourself in your profile and now charge a small fee to their clients. My guess is that people find increased value when there is a monetary commitment. That's how it is for me anyway. The goal with the redesign was that this would allow Hinge to create an online tool that allowed for more connections and increased two-way conversations among matches. The hopes are to eliminate conversations that go something like this all-too-familiar way of messaging:

Him: Hey. You're hot.
You: [silence]
Him: I like your hairstyle. I've always been attracted to brunettes.

You: [silence]
Him: Hello?
You: [silence]
Him: I was just kidding. I never go for brunettes!

Despite Hinge's redesign, there are many people who still engage in dating apps simply as a way to have fun or pass the time. Nothing more. It's just a game to them. Should it actually come to an enjoyable first date, that's merely an unexpected bonus. I don't know about you, but to me, that's pretty convincing evidence there may be a problem.

One girl told me that she gets on Hinge just to chat with guys. She'll message with them—until one of them asks her out. Once that happens, she unmatches them. Obviously, she was motivated by a desire to be wanted by men, but it didn't extend beyond that. She merely wanted to know that someone would find her attractive or desirable at first glance. She'd put herself out there on a dating app, men would respond, meeting her immediate felt need, and then she was done. I feel bad for these men. Here they are making an intentional move toward a date, and they are punished for it. Women are complicated. My friend's example may also be your motivation, but it doesn't need to be. Don't you think there are other ways to pass time that don't involve playing with people's emotions? Me too.

What are you hoping to gain on a dating app?

When you're starting mobile dating, you need to first ask yourself this: What are you hoping to gain on a dating app? If it's a sense of self-worth or a way to seek affirmation, you will be sorely disappointed. I know someone who hit a rough patch in her dating life and reloaded the dating apps she had previously deleted and sworn off (you know you've done that). She said that at first it was fun having new guys reach out to her, but then it turned into a struggle as she found herself worrying too much about how random guys viewed her profile. With her initial motivation of validation, dating apps turned into yet another avenue of insecurity.

What are your motivations? Being honest with ourselves can be hard, and sometimes we have subconscious motivations that we don't even fully understand. Not all motivations are bad, but it is important to understand yours. There is nothing wrong with being motivated to get on a dating app because you are looking to meet new people (or *any* people at all!), to broaden your dating experiences, or to grow in confidence in "putting yourself out there." Those are great motivations, normal motivations, and for those reasons I'm thankful that we have dating apps as a platform.

I do know of a few women whose sole motivation is a free meal. More than one woman has told me that she will get on a dating app because she didn't have time to grocery shop that week. I was in a conversation with a guy the other night about this very motivation. To him, that is so dishonoring. He told me that he feels used when women do this. And you know what? He's right. Women, if you are doing this, you are being disrespectful to the men. Don't use men for free meals. How would you feel if the tables were turned and the guy looked at you as a meal ticket?

Predecide Who You Will Date

Once you evaluate your motivations for dating, you can set up predecisions that make sure you don't find yourself on unnecessary dates or involved in unnecessary relationships. If you are having the same conversations repeatedly about each guy after the first date, chances are it's not them. It's you. Well, it's definitely on them that they don't have a job, but you're the one who decided to go out with them. You are the common denominator. When you return from a date and download to a girlfriend for the tenth time about how this guy doesn't have a real job, it begs the question: Did you set the expectation that having a job is important to you in the person you want to date? Obviously, if it's something you are consistently complaining about as a negative fault in the guys you've been matched with, then it's important to you. For the record, having a job is a nonnegotiable for me. And since I spend a lot of time in Nashville, working as a struggling musician when you are pushing forty doesn't cut it either. (Sorry, dreamers.)

If it's important to you, then predecide that you won't go on a date with a jobless match (or fill in the blank with whatever that expectation is for you). If you don't make the decision on the front end, you will inevitably find yourself in the same situation with the same type of guy over and over again. Have you ever heard the definition of insanity? Doing the same thing over and over again while expecting different results. My goal is to spare you from insanity while dating.

Let me tell you what I've decided before I go on a date with someone; hopefully, this will help you predecide what's most important to you in a relationship. What God says about me, others, and relationships is my go-to for how I make decisions. Jesus tells us in the gospel of Matthew that the greatest commandment is to love the Lord your God with all your heart, with all your soul, and with all your mind, and that the second greatest commandment is to love your neighbor as yourself (Matt. 22:37–39).

I take this seriously, because as Christ followers, God is telling us to prioritize him first. Not because he is arrogant or self-seeking, but because God knows that it will go better for us. God has plans for our lives that are not only good but oftentimes better than the plans we could have imagined for ourselves—and let me tell you, I can dream up some pretty incredible plans. But instead, I talk to God about my plans, and I also ask God what his plans might be, and I do my best to align the two. Jesus also tells us to love others like I'd love myself. He is not telling me—or you—to be a martyr. He is saying that, as we interact with others, we should think, "You first." When both people in the relationship have this mentality, we don't have to constantly fend for ourselves, because the other person is doing that.

What this means for me first of all is that the guy I date has to be a Christian. I don't just mean he shows up to church occasionally. I mean he has to really love Jesus and have made a conscious decision to order his life around how God tells us to live and love. That's a big deal. He also has to have a steady job and be wise with his finances. I think finances are one of those things that God has asked us to manage responsibly. Besides, I am not interested in taking on someone else's debt. In fact, I won't do it. In a perfect world, I'd ask him to prove he's contributing to a retirement fund—but I realize that may scare a few of the good ones away, so I'll restrain myself on that one. Lastly, he needs to be kind, warm, and inviting toward people. I'm not interested in someone who is rude or cold-shoulders others. Now, I realize that it will often take a date or two to discover some of these things, but because I have these decisions in place, I will know fairly early on whether or not he is a good match for me.

As you predecide your nonnegotiables for who you are and are not going to date, I would also encourage you to set yourself up for success by creating boundaries. I have a friend who made a virtual match with someone from out of state. I'm imagining some of you can relate. This particular friend is post-thirty and settled into her career, and he even more so. They agreed that'd he fly in on Friday night to meet, and he'd spend the day with her on Saturday before heading home Sunday morning. She asked him to stay in a local hotel, which was wise on her end. By the time the waiter poured the water at the restaurant on Friday evening, it was clear he was very much interested in my friend. My friend, however, did not reciprocate. Not even a tiny bit. And yet she still had a full day ahead of her with this guy. She is polite, responsible, and engaging, so she was willing to roll with the punches the next day despite how painful it felt. Let's just say he wanted to begin a committed relationship right then and there. She more or less told him that they'd never be seeing each other again. Have a nice flight home.

That's an extreme example, I realize, but a word to the wise: predecide your time constraints before you find yourself in a similar situation. If it's a first date, you don't need to take a two-hour drive each direction to see the meteor shower in the Rocky Mountains. A dinner, coffee, or casual round of miniature golf will probably do the trick. Think through what a timeline looks like for you so that you will be most comfortable, and predecide.

Don't Be Confused

When we're weighing our motivations and trying to make healthy predecisions about our dating lives, sometimes we confuse what we want in the short term with what's most important to us ultimately. For example, as girls, we naturally want to be loved, honored, and adored. Every girl wants to feel beautiful, and we often look to men to affirm that in us. We love getting attention from guys because it makes us feel important, valuable, and wanted. Dating apps can provide these things.

However, there is also the potential for dating apps to tempt us to compromise our long-term goals for temporary gratification. In other words, we may want long-term companionship, but we will go out with a guy we wouldn't otherwise be interested in, merely because he showed interest in us and because we're feeling lonely. This is completely understandable, so if you have found yourself in this position, it's okay. Pick yourself back up and try again. It's never too late to start fresh.

Still, this is also why I am so adamant about defining your motivations and predecisions on the front end. I don't want you to confuse a natural desire for long-term companionship with a need for instant satisfaction. If you don't love yourself first, a relationship won't be able to fix that for you. There is an element of not wasting your time or his, for that matter, when it's clear you have no intention of taking it beyond date number one.

Disclaimer: Here is what I'm not saying. I am not saying never give guys a chance. That would be ridiculous. How many people do you know who are happily married whose stories go something like this, "After our first date, I wasn't all that interested, but something led me to say yes a second time. It was on date number two that something changed. I got to know him differently, and the rest is history." We can all recount some version of a story like that. What I am saying is that you need to know generally what you are looking for before you engage in a dating app. When you know what you're looking for, it's easy to say no to the guys who won't be a great match for you. Let's just all spare ourselves from the aftermath and comments from our girlfriends that go something like this: "Why would you even think to go out with a guy like that?"

Here is a small caveat. It's one thing to draw appropriate lines in the sand and it's another thing to eliminate possibilities altogether. There is naturally some risk in dating, as in most things in life. Not to sidetrack us, but have you ever been "catfished"? Someone put forth the ideal online profile to lure you in, and once you met up, he could not be more opposite from his online persona. Yep, that happens. It's a risk we all take when beginning our relationships virtually. It comes with the territory, unfortunately.

Both single men and women have told me that once they set their general parameters for dating, they would say yes to anyone who fell into that category. Both sexes cited two main reasons. First, even if you are not a perfect match once you meet in person, there is always an opportunity to learn something. You can learn something about yourself, about the other person, or more about what you are or are not looking for. And second, you never know who their friends are and if one of their friends would be a great match for you. Set your expectations and define a few of your nonnegotiables and remember— no one is perfect. You're not, so don't expect him to be either.

Under No Obligation

Predecisions aren't only about long-term and short-term expectations for your match; they are also about your expectations for yourself. One of the most important predecisions you can make is to predecide that it's okay to say no. In conversations with single women of all ages, I've found a common prevailing thought among many of them. The thought goes something like this: If a single guy asks you out, even over an app, you owe it to them to say yes. The reasoning seems rather simple to the girl. Because he has gotten up the nerve to directly ask if you'd spend time with him, you are now obligated to say yes.

What? No one has forced this man to ask you on a date, and no one is forcing you to respond favorably. You do have a responsibility, however, to be clear and kind in your response. But you are certainly under no obligation to say yes. Some girls are inclined to feel a certain level of guilt for not wanting to go out with someone, or they think they'll hurt the guy's feelings if they decline. And maybe the guy *will* have hurt feelings, but it's only temporary. Do you know what is even more hurtful? Saying yes outwardly when inwardly it's a no, or passively making up excuses as to why you're busy, fully knowing there will never come a time when you are not "busy."

This is a reality of dating apps that needs to be addressed. When a guy you are no longer interested in engages with you, you swipe left. It's as simple as that. No more conversation needed. You can ignore him, delete him, or whatever form of moving on that you choose, and that's the end of it. Whether mid conversation or not, you can, with one subtle movement of your thumb, pretend as though he never existed.

Until you are rematched on a different dating app, that is. Let's face it, you and I both know the likelihood of that happening is fairly high.

What I'm suggesting—which may be incredibly unpopular to several of you—is if you've at minimum selected one another and had some level of back-and-forth dialogue, will you predecide to kindly decline before ghosting on him? A simple, "Thank you, but I don't think you are what I'm looking for. I wish you the best," is sufficient. That's it. Move on. Your argument may be, "But these guys have never interacted with me with that level of respect!" I believe you. Trust me, you have no idea how much I believe you. With that being said, we can still model something different and more kind. There is no harm in being polite.

A friend of mine gave a great leadership talk on how to be clear and kind in communication, and the same principles apply to dating. Because, truthfully, someone needs to have a level of maturity and lead well in dating. Sometimes that will be you. Guys use all sorts of appropriate, inappropriate, and everything-in-between pickup lines to start the communicating. Granted, we've all gotten those incoming messages where we thought, "Okay, buddy, you definitely crossed the line with that one. Goodbye." I'm not talking about those. I am talking about the pickup lines that come across our screens that are mildly cheesy and may cause us to slightly raise our eyebrows. The context is that he's not someone we'd be attracted to, so it makes the line that much worse. I know a few people who, if there were a course in "How to Give Snarky and Rude Comebacks," could teach the class. I'm going to encourage you to respond differently.

As a follower of Jesus, loving people should be a priority. In general, I think we'd all agree that if everyone did just that one thing, the world would be a significantly better place. But it's hard. I get it. However, I think we still need to try. Loving people does not mean that you have to say yes to every guy who asks you out. You should probably be clear and kind, though. In other words, tell him directly you are not interested and don't be rude about it. When you are unclear and unkind, not only is it confusing, but you are only modeling his rude comment back to him. When you are unclear but kind, he is flat-out confused and will possibly keep after you until you block him. And when you are clear but unkind, it just reflects poorly on you. It is not doing anyone any favors when you say, "No, thank you, you're ugly." The next time you get messaged by someone you're not interested in, try being clear and kind.

Final Caution

I've already mentioned the three things that are absolute nonnegotiables for me in someone I'd date. There is a list (okay, maybe a long list) of other things that are preferences, but at the end of the day are not deal breakers. However, since I know that there are a few things I will not bend on, I do not go on dates or get involved long term with anyone who falls outside those parameters. The reason being that it is unfair of me to justify away things that are core values of mine, and it is unfair to put expectations on someone else that he may change for you. It's also not worth the heartbreak on my end, or his, to emotionally get involved while knowing that it cannot turn into a long-term relationship.

 It is unfair to put expectations on someone else that he may change for you.

My word of caution is similar for you. Once you've decided what your deal breakers are, stick to them. Do not allow yourself to rationalize away something that is extremely important to you because you've convinced yourself that he might change. He might change, but that needs to happen without you in the picture.

Questions for Reflection

1. What were your motivations for getting on a dating app? After reading this chapter, are there areas where you may need to adjust your motivations?
2. Have you ever compromised your long-term goals for short-term satisfaction in a relationship? What happened? What did you learn about what you are looking for in a relationship?
3. Think through some predecisions you can make as you look for a person you'd want to date. If it's helpful, write them down.

When to Swipe Left

Once you know what you're looking for in a relationship, it's easy to spot the guys who don't fit. Well, at least it should be. One of the more challenging things about dating apps is that it's more common for women to take them seriously than it is for men. What do I mean by that? Of all the conversations I've had about dating apps, there were some themes that repeatedly cropped up. Women, in general, are motivated to download an app of their choosing because they are genuinely interested in meeting a great guy, hoping that it might turn into a healthy relationship. Men are more likely to download an app, sit side by side with their buddies in the living room, and swipe as fast as they can. May the best man win. To be fair, men and women are still equal opportunity offenders—both positively and negatively. But since I'm talking to the women here, how do you recognize when a man is doing this? I want you to know what the red flags are from men you may not want to get involved with, so you can make that decision for yourself once you see them—both on the app and on the first date.

My desire for you is that you would find a man who treats you with the honor and respect you deserve. You have every right to expect nothing less than that. When we are first getting to know someone, particularly if we find him attractive and he reciprocates, we can talk ourselves into thinking his less-than-ideal behaviors are "not that bad." It's better to pay attention to these things on the front end of getting to know someone, rather than after you have weeks or even

months invested in the relationship. By that time, our emotions may be really involved and our justifications tend to outweigh our rationale.

Profiles and Messaging

With dating apps, a guy's profile is the first thing you'll see about him, and already there can be good signs and not-so-good signs. Different women place varying levels of importance on their own profiles. Some go with the route that less is more, and others max out the allotted characters. That's your call and you need to define what that looks like for you. It is worth mentioning though, that if you fall in the camp of "very important that you read my profile," I wouldn't easily justify those who you've matched with who clearly didn't follow your preference. It's not necessarily a red flag, but it's at least worth a raised eyebrow. For instance, if you make a definitive statement about no hookups and his opening line is a request to meet up at his place tonight, this is not the guy you're looking for. My hope is that this is not the guy anyone is looking for.

One of the reasons that profiles can be hard to navigate is that people can pretend to be whoever they want while hiding behind their devices. Profiles don't always tell the truth. But there are a few dead giveaways that may be worth an immediate swipe left. As I had continuing conversations with both single men and women about absolute no-no's on profiles, here is what rose to the top. An assorted arrangement of mirror selfies, pictures with so many friends that it's hard to tell which one he is, and wedding pictures. That's right, wedding pictures. I'm not entirely sure why he thinks that a shot of him and his (hopefully) ex-wife is going to net a match. Apparently, it's working for him or I'd have to think he would have changed his strategy. So ladies, please, don't encourage that.

On a personal note, if a guy's entire profile is exclusively a library of his selfies, then I'm going to think one of two things. He has no friends, because if he did, surely one of them could have snapped a shot. Or, he is a narcissist. Both of which are definitely getting the swipe left. You can make your own decision on which direction you'll swipe, but file that thought away for the next time you're scrolling.

Another giant red flag is a profile that reads, "My girlfriend and I are on a break" or "My girlfriend and I are both on here." Swipe left. Move on.

Most girls I've talked with stated that when they see a guy with an empty bio, more often than not it can mean he is from out of town and looking for a meet-up. Not a date. Not a relationship. A "meet-up." Of course, this is not a rule, but merely something to keep in mind, and strictly based on conversations I've had with women who've learned that lesson the hard way. If your intent is to find an actual relationship, the empty-profile guy is most likely not taking the app seriously and is not the best match for you.

When he sends the same message he sent to your friend, that's also an instant, "No, thank you." You should expect a guy to do more than just copy and paste the same line to girl after girl. I'd encourage you to go for a guy who is willing to invest more effort than that. This is also an indicator he may only be looking for a "good time."

There does tend to be a strategy for profile pictures. It goes something like this: one serious, one funny to show your personality, and one with your friends to show you have friends. If you have a relationship with your family, that pic is included too. Browsing profiles, you'll also come across the shirtless selfie pic, the weightlifting pic, the pic with a dog, the pic where the dog is covering his face, and the pic displaying his most recent kill of ducks, deer, doves, or fish. These tell you a lot about a guy, although what's bad for you may be good for someone else. Just be sure you know what you're looking for.

First Dates

First dates are an interesting thing, especially within the context of our current culture. Some of you remember when dating happened differently than it does now, and others of you just have to imagine it. But dates used to happen as a result of an in-person connection. The most complicated part of the process for me was deciding which pair of shoes to wear before he arrived at my door. Because of my interactions with him prior to saying yes, the red flags were more obvious and, in my opinion, easier to navigate.

We don't really see first dates happening like that as much. Don't get me wrong, sometimes they do—and if I'm being honest, I wish more of them still would. More often, it seems that first dates are a result of a click from a notification on your phone screen. Inside is a message, "Want to meet tonight at 7?" Or to make matters worse, you've been messaging back and forth for a few days. He finally texts, "We should go to coffee or something." There's the bait. How will you respond? You think to yourself, "Well, obviously we're going to end up as electronic pen pals if I don't respond more directly." You type out, "How about this Saturday afternoon at 2? There's a great coffee spot in my neighborhood." It's annoying, really. Why couldn't he have done that? But, whatever. He seems cute. In fact, really cute. He's put together and has a compatible profile, and you're free. You say yes and show up. Or in the latter example, he says yes and you show up.

This is a situation that a friend of mine found herself in. (My guess is that some of you have had this same experience.) Here is my bit of advice: if you want a guy who is willing to initiate or make the first move, then his lack of initiative should be a red flag. In that case, move on. Your protest may be, "How will I ever get a date if I don't initiate?" That's a fair question. But I have spoken to plenty of single men who have said to me that they will rise to the standard set for them. If they are interested in a girl, they will meet whatever standard she has set to date her. In other words, if you've made it known you expect him to take the initiative and he doesn't step up, that's a red flag.

Beginning conversations virtually not only makes it harder to read people but it has a unique set of challenges as well. Because of the changes in technology, which have moved us from in-person to online meetings, I'd argue that the younger generations are being conditioned to emotionally connect virtually. It's a learned behavior that Generation X didn't grow up with (and Baby Boomers struggle to comprehend). Millennials and the generations after them do not know life without smartphones and the World Wide Web in their pockets. When we connect emotionally without ever meeting someone in person, the danger is that we've created a counterfeit relationship. We don't really know what it's like to watch him react to situations, interact with other people in real time, or navigate basic life issues. The only thing we know is an idealistic version presented to us on a screen, and our imaginations fill in the gaps with the information we prefer.

This is why it's important to spend time interacting in real life. I realize that electronic communication is not going away. Besides, I think it's a brilliant technological advancement. Calling on the phone can be so boring when I can instead send a bitmoji that keeps up with both current events and fashion trends. By the way, bitmojis are more similar to dating app profiles than we realize. They were created to be personalized avatars, reflecting your appearance and personality. And they do. Well, the absolute, picture-perfect, photoshopped, how-I-wish-I-really-looked version. Not all that different from most of our dating profiles.

Here are a few things to pay attention to on a first date. You may think some of these should go without saying, but there is a reason it's worth listing them.

1. *Is he being rude to the waitstaff?* He was kind and polite via text, over the phone, and once you arrived in person. You walked up to the counter to order a cup of coffee, or sat down at a table to look over the menu. Someone approaches you to take your order. If he speaks to them in a belittling, demeaning, or a less-than-congenial sort of way, I'd consider that a red flag. I can hear some of you now. You think I'm overreacting. For me, not being interested in someone who is rude to a server is not overreacting. Everyone has inherent value, and everyone deserves our respect. God has designed it to be that way. God did not create certain people better than other people. We may all have different jobs, skills, hobbies, or interests, but that is what we do. It is not who we are. No one should be mistreated. Personally, I have a low tolerance for that.

2. *Is he checking his phone the whole time?* Thirty minutes without our phones won't kill us. It certainly won't kill him. It's challenging to

get to know someone when he is more interested in whatever is going on on his phone than he is in you. I have been on several dates with men who text and check social media nonstop. I have even been in a relationship with someone like that. I did not learn the lesson when I first noticed it. There was something in me that believed either it wasn't a big deal or he'd stop. It was a big deal and he never stopped. Nine times out of ten, he won't change. For me, I feel devalued when I'm consistently interrupted because he needs to respond to a text or look at whatever new post popped up on his newsfeed. Facebook— *really*? If that is more engaging than a conversation with you, you both could have stayed home for that. (In case you missed it, they now have a name for this: phubbing. In other words, someone paying so much attention to their phone they essentially snub their date.)

3. *Is he only talking about himself?* There is a thin line between being proud of his achievements and accomplishments and finding a way to turn every topic of conversation into a story about him. If he is only interested in himself now, he will only be interested in himself in the future. One of the more obvious signs of narcissism is when he has a way of comparing everything you've mentioned with some better version of the story in his life. Your first date isn't supposed to be about one-upping each other. When he is no longer sharing a charming "me too" story, then it's clearly an issue of arrogance. I'd go ahead and swipe left on date number two.

4. *Is he bringing up his ex?* It's a first date. There is no need to bring up past relationships. On a first date, this is a warning sign because this means he is either not in a position to date someone new or he is already comparing you to his last relationship. First dates should be considered as blank slates. It's important that he does the work to minimize the emotional baggage before starting something new. The same goes for you, I might add.

5. *Is he moving too fast?* You just met the guy and you've commit-ted to nothing outside of the minutes that form the parameters of

this lunch, dinner, or cup of coffee. If he starts talking about meeting your parents, getting married, or having kids, be careful. Additionally, men will say just about anything to get a woman in bed. If you've been on dating apps of any kind, you've already encountered this. Yes, even the Christian dating apps! The kind of guy you're looking for will have appropriate boundaries and be respectful of yours.

6. *Is he married?* I hate that I even have to add this to the list, but I do. I have had one too many girlfriends end up on first dates with seemingly respectable men, and the first question out of his mouth once they are in person is, "I need to let you know that I'm married; is that going to be a problem?" I cannot make this stuff up. Walk away. Do not hesitate with this one. Do not engage any further in the conversation. It will never be worth it.

First Dates Live

Last night, I was sitting with a group of twentysomething single girls, talking about first date experiences. One girl talked about a guy she matched with on one of the apps. She replayed how their initial messaging went. They texted back and forth for a few weeks before he asked if she'd like to spend a Saturday afternoon at the Nashville Zoo. She was excited because she was looking forward to getting to know this guy more. They had a good connection, she said, and she had enjoyed their initial banter. Although they had never spoken, not even on the phone, her account went something like this: "I met this guy, we talked, had a good connection, and then he asked me out." Those are probably not the words I would have chosen to describe the situation, had it been me. I don't typically equate texting with talking or app-matching with meeting. Those are words I reserve for in-person encounters. However, this does illustrate the ways that matches can cause our mind to create fictitious relationships. But I was following her.

When the two of them finally met in person, she was disappointed. That initial connection she thought they had fell flat. Nothing. He was a fine young man, but his personality was deader than a door-knob. He wasn't even someone she'd be friends with. Physically, he was incredibly attractive, but nothing more.

 If you don't want to be friends with the guy, you're certainly not going to enjoy being in a relationship with him.

This brings up an important point. If you don't want to be friends with the guy, you're certainly not going to enjoy being in a relationship with him. I don't care how cute the guy is, if you're bored to tears, it won't work. Thank him for the nice time and swipe left. This is not one of those times where you talk yourself into it. There will be a lot of times where you will be a perfect match for someone on paper, but if you cannot connect in person, which is where real relationships live, let it go.

There will also be dates that start off well and you'll start thinking, "This definitely has potential for date number two." And then it happens. He chews with his mouth open. Pops his jaw. Cracks his knuckles. Or maybe he has shifty eyes. A lot of people have trouble maintaining eye contact, particularly when they are nervous or just meeting someone. But here's the thing with eyes: you both have them and it can be annoying when he never looks at yours, and instead appears to be constantly scanning the room for a hostile takeover. Or worse, his eyes tend to land on every other girl in the room but you. Jitters can also be normal. But if his jitters cause you to believe he has restless legs syndrome, or that he may be trying to detox from a drug addiction, that can be a little much. The bottom line: if he has mannerisms and idiosyncrasies that you can't stand now, those things will only be exponentially magnified on subsequent dates. That may be worth swiping left.

I know of someone who went on a Hinge date. They met at a local pub for a casual dinner. About halfway into their time together, she realized he was trying to sell her insurance. When your date turns into a sales pitch, it's probably time to move on.

This happened to me recently. I connected with a guy, and after forty-five minutes of conversation, I realized he was only interested in providing refinancing for my loans. Unfortunately for him, I don't have loans—or debt. Unfortunately for me, I was a sales opportunity to him, not a date. Some people are entertained by stories like these. I know I am—as long as they don't involve me. Regardless, if you are looking for a real connection, you can check the guy off your list as soon as he turns you into a potential client.

Such mini catastrophes bring up the need for a couple of helpful reminders for a first date.

1. *Take your own car.* I was tempted not to mention this, because people rarely get picked up for a first date by someone they've matched with on a dating app. But many girls still hold to the standard that the man should pick them up for a date, and under other circumstances, that's a personal preference of mine as well. Despite what older generations may think, chivalry is not dead. It may be aging quicker than us single women would prefer, but with enough nudging, I feel confident we can resurrect it. (We'll save that for chapter 8, though.)

In these circumstances, though, he's still a stranger. This is where the rule comes in that most of us were taught as children, "Don't get into the car of a stranger." If you had any doubts, I hope I've pushed you toward the direction of taking your own car. Besides, if this guy ends up being less interesting than a washed-up piece of driftwood at the beach, you'll have your own escape route. You will no longer be held captive to his seemingly endless tales of rock polishing, insect collecting, or how he recently got into composting in his backyard. It's a first date, people: bring your A game.

Worse yet is if he can't stop talking and his topic of choice is himself. I am a huge fan of learning about others, but there is a difference between healthy dialogue between two people as they try to get to know each other and a 120-minute monologue without coming up for air. At that point, you could probably just get up and leave and he'd never even notice. So again, take your own car. It's better to be safe.

2. *Don't give him your address.* Not before you've met him, that is. If there is a date number two, then by all means go for it. Hopefully, he *will* pick you up! However, there is no need to prematurely tell him you live alone in the only yellow house on Strawberry Lane. Or recount, in your initial messaging, the number of times you've locked yourself out of the house—but not to worry, you now have a spare key underneath the second potted plant in the backyard. Some private information needs to stay private.

These are two tips that are easy to implement, and having your own car is the fastest way to swipe left mid date and abort mission.

Digital Bread Crumbs

Whether you're talking to guys you are interested in dating or guys you've dated in the past, another red flag to watch for is "breadcrumbing." Breadcrumbing is when one person sends out flirtatious but noncommittal messages, either through social media or text just often enough to keep you interested, but not frequently enough to put any deposit into the relationship. In other words, if he senses that you may move on and forget about him, he'll send you a digital bread crumb to remind you that he's still there.

This can look like a lot of things. Some of the more obvious bread crumbs are likes on an Instagram photo that is several weeks old, not to mention that you have not heard from him in months. Why? He knows you are about to forget about him, so he'll slide into your DM or tag you in something, seizing the opportunity to make you turn your attention toward him. It's interesting to note that leaving you digital bread crumbs takes serious strategy on his end. If only he had put this much effort and intentionality into dating you. As tempting as it may be, swipe left.

You've probably known a breadcrumber. I have. His messages are sporadic, with just enough content to pique your interest, but not enough to give you any sort of clarity about his intentions. Bread-crumbing falls somewhere in between ghosting and a slow fade. They don't instantaneously vanish on you, but they also don't slowly remove themselves from the picture over time. Instead, they are incredibly inconsistent and incredibly annoying.

A real man won't play digital games with you.

The most common form of breadcrumbing that I've encountered is from the guy who has flirted with me, both in person and digitally, but never makes a committed move. Yet every month or so, he'll "love" my new profile pic or some random picture from last year—which had to take some serious digging to find, I might add. As women, this toys with our emotions. Particularly if this is a guy we would have been interested in. It reignites the what-ifs all over again. To me, however, this is selfish on the guy's part. His contact is intermittent and vague for a reason: he wants to keep you as an option. Women, don't fall for it. A real man won't play digital games with you. As best you can, delete the messages and move on.

You Too

Dating is a two-way street, and it's unfair to put all the weight and responsibility of dating on men. As women, we need to take owner-ship too. It's worth mentioning that in the hundreds of conversations I've had with both single men and women about dating, these were behaviors and characteristics that were a swipe left for men as well.

Breadcrumbing, for example, is not exclusive to men. Women do this all the time. Have you ever found yourself wondering if the guy you like is dating anyone? You scroll through his social media; one thing leads to another and you find yourself looking at pictures and comments from eight months back. It doesn't hurt to throw out a com-ment or leave a heart behind, right? Maybe let him know you're still out there and paying attention to him? Listen, that's breadcrumbing.

Now you're the one who is doing it. If he is not paying attention to you currently, resist the urge to play games and try to lure him back in. You don't want to settle for the guy that you had to convince to like you, or the guy that you had to remind that you're still available. If he is interested, he won't need to be convinced.

Each of us has unique mannerisms and habits. Some of them are weird; others are barely noticeable. Personally, I will only eat M&M's if they are frozen. I know it's odd, but it's my preference. However, I don't anticipate this being a deal breaker for someone. But you and I may have things in our lives that could be deal breakers for a guy, and we don't even realize it. Overwhelming a guy with your preferred baby names is probably not your best move on date number one. Neither is making fun of his career of choice. If you don't like something about him, that's okay. Just keep it to yourself. That's why we need to have people in our lives who can gently reflect our nuances back to us. These things could be preventing us from finding a great guy and we don't even realize it.

Questions for Reflection

1. What characteristics would cause you to swipe left on someone?
2. Have you ever tried to be someone you're not on a dating app? What weren't you telling the whole truth about? Have you experienced men projecting a different version of themselves online that you didn't discover was false until meeting them in person?
3. Have you been the recipient of digital bread crumbs, or left them for a guy? How did that make you feel?

Options, Part 1: Optionitis

One of the most powerful words in the human vocabulary is *no*. Do you ever have a hard time saying that word? For some of you, it feels on par with the four-letter words your parents told you not to say when you were growing up. However, this word only has two letters. So why does it feel like it packs such a punch?

There were many years of my life where I could not empathize with people who had trouble with this phrase. For me, the word *no* would roll too easily off my tongue, as easily as my own name. In fact, I felt more in tune with Meghan Trainor. If you have no idea what I'm talking about, google some of her hit songs from 2016. You'll get it. People-pleasing was never my thing and I had great mentors in my life who taught me about boundaries fairly early on. Unless it was M&M's. It was, and still is, a rare day when I pass up those small candy-coated bites of chocolate heaven. In fact, I have poured myself a small bowl of dark chocolate M&M's before beginning each chapter of this book. My loyalty runs deep.

I'm guessing for you, there are plenty of times when you've wondered how the word *yes* came out of your mouth when you were so loudly saying the opposite in your head. Maybe it was watching your friend's dog when you secretly hate animals or going to a concert on a work night that you were only semi-interested in. There is the flip side of this too. Saying no when your alarm goes off at five in the morning but your body gets up anyway and miraculously ends up at the gym. There are times when saying no is both a good and bad

There
can be freedom
in saying no.

thing. And if this is a word that makes an infrequent appearance in your vocabulary, I'd suggest you become more familiar with it. There can be freedom in saying no.

The reason is this: Haven't you been in a situation where you now look back and think, "Why didn't I just say no?" It could be as simple as that time you said yes to a second date that you didn't really want to be on. Instead of enjoying yourself, you spent the first half of the date trying to come up with a reason as to why you suddenly "had to leave." Or it could be something more consequential. You either got involved with someone or stayed in a relationship with someone *way beyond* the breaking point. I've done that. *Why didn't I say no sooner? What in the world was I thinking?*

Hindsight is always twenty-twenty. For me, I tend to relive the moments that were clear warning signs and wonder why I didn't say no and end it at the time. But the truth is that I know why I didn't say no. I suspect that to some degree you know why you didn't say no either. For me, it was a combination of not recognizing that I had a choice in whether or not I wanted to be in the relationship, and justifying the warning signs that I might just be an option. Either of those things alone can derail you when gotten out of hand, but the combination of the two are a recipe for disaster and then some. I want you to be aware of when you are being treated as an option and to feel equipped to say no to the guy who treats you as one.

Decisions and Optionitis

Saying yes or no is a choice you get to make, and in a relationship you will have to choose to say yes or no over and over again. In the same way he chose to swipe right on you, you chose to swipe right on him. Relationships don't happen by accident. You don't accidentally show up on a first date or a fourth date, meet his parents, or exchange Christmas gifts. In the same way we choose to show up to our job, pay our bills, and put gas in our car when it's empty, being in a relationship is a choice. You either choose to be in or you choose to be out. Even under the most ideal circumstances, you are still making a choice. As a side note: marriages work this way too. Long after the wedding vows, both husband and wife make the choice to love the other person.

Dating apps have introduced even more choices in how we date and who we date. And unfortunately, infinite choices can lead to endless swiping. That's the reality of the world we live in. An unfortunate by-product of the dating app era is "optionitis." Optionitis is a disease (that I made up) where men are unable to make a decision due to too many options. This results in men choosing all the women on their phone instead of just one, which essentially means he has chosen no one. Have you ever sat at a table with a guy you met on a dating app and while you were with him, he tried to discreetly pull out his phone and continue the swiping? Optionitis. FOBO is real and lots of men have it. *FOBO* is fear of better options, in case you're hearing that term for the first time, but I doubt it. Unfortunately.

I have sat eye to eye with men who have had track records of dating some of the most quality women I've ever met, and I asked these guys why their various relationships ended. What went wrong, I wondered? Most of the men had similar remarks. But to quote one of them, he said, "I'm afraid that if I choose her, someone better will come along, and then I'll regret making the wrong choice." Mic drop! There it is. FOBO in action. The truth is that men are already predisposed to this fear. It's not as though dating apps created a new fear in men. Unfortunately, though, dating apps put a spotlight on it, publicizing what was once more private. (It is important to note, however, that there will be times when there *is* a better option. In chapter 8, we will talk about what those relationships will look like.)

It's so important to understand your role in making decisions about your relationships, because if need be, you will end the relationship by making a choice. No one can do that for you. Only you can decide for yourself. I had to learn this the hard way. Do you remember when I said at the beginning of this chapter that I had a hard time empathizing with people who struggled with saying no? A few relationships taught me otherwise. I had allowed someone to take up emotional residence in my life, so I justified his behavior because it felt better than the alternative, which was being alone.

Not all my relationships were bad, and not all of them were all bad. There were great moments in the relationships and great qualities in these guys. But I had made the choice to stay involved longer than I should have, causing heartache beyond belief. Hopefully by sharing some of my experiences, it will prevent some of you from ending up in similar situations.

I remember when I had finally made the choice to end a relationship. The last six months had been volatile. When I say volatile, I mean on some days he was kind, caring, and attentive, and on other days he gave me the silent treatment or short, rude responses. As soon as I thought I could predict him—or us—something would change on a dime. I knew this relationship needed to come to a close. One night, an hour before I was to go meet him, I found myself on my knees in my bedroom, begging God for clarity. I don't know how to describe what I heard that night since it wasn't an audible voice, but I know I heard God say, "Let him go." It was so clear to me in that moment: I needed to let him and this relationship go. But I didn't. I began to convince myself that the good still outweighed the bad, and that maybe the bad wasn't really *that bad*. That decision led to six of some of the most difficult months of my adult life.

 I don't need to settle for being someone's option because the right guy will make me his priority.

I was out of town during the final conversation that put the nail in the coffin of our relationship. I was at a conference, in fact, and I needed to somehow pull myself back together to walk into the event space. I sat in my car after hanging up with him, and it hit me like a ton of bricks. Everything from the past several months of this relationship became so clear to me: *I was just an option to him.* He was only interested in me when it was convenient for him, when he had nothing else to do, and when no other girl was vying for his attention.

That was all I was ever going to be. An option. And when he no longer needed me as an option, he moved on. Things I never understood in our relationship became clear in that moment. Conversations and interactions that I could never quite make sense of took on alarming clarity. I felt incredibly dumb. All the red flags were there, waving in my face, and I had dismissed them. Have you ever been in that situation? Just as I was about to get out of my car to walk into the building for the next session, I thought, *I don't need to settle for being someone's option because the right guy will make me his priority.* I deserve that. So do you.

Warning Signs

You may be wondering: "What were the warning signs? How do I recognize if I'm being treated as someone's option?" There are a number of ways, but here are some of the more obvious ones. If you experience any of these, you need to say no and move on.

1. *What time of day is he texting you?* This question is valid whether you are four days, four weeks, or four months into the relationship. Be very careful if you regularly receive messages from him after ten or eleven at night. In my personal experience, and in the experiences of many women I've spoken with, texts that show up on your phone near the midnight hour should serve as a caution. Typically, this means he's bored. Don't assume after-hours texts equal a genuine, selfless interest in you. Before you dispute that sentence, here is what I'm not saying: I am not saying sending late-night text messages is bad. What I am pointing out, however, is that if he *only* sends you messages during this time frame, you may just be an option.

During the rocky six months of our relationship, I would sporadically see a "hey" or "you awake?" show up on my phone between eleven and one at night. He almost never texted me outside of this time frame. I wasn't always awake during this time, but when I was, I did what most girls do. I responded. And then I engaged in an hour-long text exchange in the middle of the night when I should have been sleeping. But I dismissed the hour of day and rationalized it by thinking, *This is the only time he can connect with me.* It's true. I really did think that.

There was another guy that I was getting to know over the course of several months. We were not exclusive, at least we'd never had any sort of DTR chat. But we had each verbally communicated to the other person our level of interest and attraction. He was also someone with the habit of texting me in the middle of the night. What I didn't realize, and came to find out later, was that he was doing this to other girls as well. At the same time. His line of work caused him to work late at night and into the early hours of the morning, and even when he wasn't working, he would still be awake.

I once heard him talk about those hours being the time he struggled most with being single. I should have gotten a clue right then and there. I didn't. It turned out as long as he was keeping himself busy, he was content. But when he found himself with space in his schedule, he resorted to going through the list of girls on his phone, looking for someone to fill the void. He started texting in the middle of the night, putting out the bait, and seeing who would respond. He just needed an option. I happened to be that for him, and I had no idea.

2. *Does everything revolve around his schedule?* He makes the plans and they usually hatch at the last minute. Maybe you've found yourself justifying his behavior because earlier in the week, he asked you about your schedule. But it stopped there. He knew what you were doing and still didn't make any plans with you. In turn, you found yourself turning down other invites or not making any plans at all, hoping and waiting to see if he would circle back around with you. But he doesn't. And when he doesn't, you feel stupid that you just wasted a night. When he does show up, he gives you two hours' notice at best that he's available. Because that's what works for him. So, of course, you make it work too. Time together needs to be more than when it's convenient for him. If he is thinking exclusively about what works for him and not taking your schedule into account, you may just be an option.

I still remember one of the last times this happened to me. It was a Friday afternoon and a text came through. He wanted to borrow a few ministry resources that I had. As a side note, I have been working in large churches around the country for the past two decades. By default, most of the guys I've been in relationships with have been, in some capacity, associated with the organization I worked with. There have been times this has caused the lines between our professional and personal worlds to blur. This was one of those times. I replied to the text and told him yes. The catch was that he could only meet me downtown at six o'clock that night. Did I mention this was Friday night?

Believe it or not, this was one of those times I had already decided to just go ahead and make plans with a girlfriend. So, of course, I canceled. I rearranged a few other things so I could actually fight my way through rush hour on time, and drove to meet him. He arrived late, so I waited. We spent about thirty minutes together catching up before he had to leave. I silenced the warning signals because, after all, he could have asked anyone else, but he chose me. Clearly, he wanted to spend time with me, however short our meeting. In those few minutes, he said everything I wanted to hear. How much he appreciated me, how thankful he was that I was in his life. After the fact, I discovered that he was borrowing the resources from me to take into a meeting later that night. A "meeting" that involved helping a girl he was interested in. He used me. He knew that when he said to jump, I would ask how high. He wasn't interested in me. He was interested in what I could offer. I was just an option.

3. *Does he listen to you?* You remember everything he tells you about his life, and he has told you a lot. You know all about his work and his family and how he spends his free time. You've paid attention to his mannerisms, his quirks, and even his insecurities. You feel valued that he would share so much with you, and the fact that you are the one he calls to celebrate the small victories in the day speaks volumes about your relationship. Things are going well. Until you realize he doesn't remember anything you say. At first it's no big deal. There are plenty of times you have forgotten something that someone told you.

Then you realize that whenever the topic of conversation turns to
you, you see the glazed look come over his eyes as he is clearly thinking about something other than what is coming out of your mouth.

I spent several months with someone like this. We had a great
time together; it was fun and full of energy, and there were very few
people who I would consistently laugh that hard with. It was a relationship that felt life-giving. I was in a difficult season in my job and
our relationship provided a needed distraction from my day-to-day
challenges. Things seemed to be headed in a positive direction—until
I realized that he knew nothing about me. Not because I didn't share.
I did plenty of talking. But he never listened. I didn't pick up on it at
first, because it's not my natural inclination to question whether I'm
being heard when I talk. Especially not in this context.

Initially, I noticed him asking questions about things we had previously discussed at length. As silly as this sounds, when I finally put
two and two together, I realized that he didn't even know if I had
any siblings or where I was from. He had never asked me anything
personal about my life. He wasn't interested because there was no
benefit for him. The fun that we had together was an outlet for him
as well because he too was in a heavy season in life. The difference?
I was emotionally invested and he was not. I was just a convenient
option.

4. *Are you making excuses for him?* Your friends or family question
his interactions with you, and you find yourself spewing out the same
excuses that he gave you. The worst part is that even if you don't
believe him, you still defend him because it's embarrassing to think
that you were played for a fool. When you are together, you ask him
about it. That's what healthy relationships look like. When there are
gaps in a relationship, you have conversation so that you can bridge
the gap with truth instead of whatever you've made up in your mind
about the situation or other person.

He accuses you of being crazy. But you're not. Hear me, girls: You
are never crazy to stand up for yourself. You are worthy, valuable,
and don't need to justify your feelings. Your feelings are your feelings,

and no one should ever make you feel crazy for feeling or thinking a certain way. Silently, you still hold on to those few moments that are good, and hope that something may change. But deep down, you know you shouldn't be treated this way. He is treating you as an option.

Perhaps you've even gotten up the nerve to tell him no and move on. You thought he heard you. In your mind, it was over. And then he reappeared. Be wary of the guy who tries to keep a hook on you when you move toward ending the relationship. At the risk of sounding like a broken record, you are not an option.

If you are currently in a relationship with these warning signs, I'd encourage you to move on. It's hard. I know that all too well. Remember? I lived in a relationship like that far past the expiration date. But sometimes the hard thing and the right thing are the same thing. The right thing may hurt at the time, but you won't regret it. The wrong thing usually has a shadow of regret.

I never wanted to be the poster child for how hard it can be to say no. It's embarrassing. But it's real. I am not the only person who has had these experiences. My goal is to prevent you from finding yourself stuck in a trap of someone else's optionitis. Why was it so hard for me to say no at the time? I was emotionally involved and allowed this to cloud what I thought I wanted and deserved. But "no" would have been the best word that could have come out of my mouth. I was giving the wrong person emotional real estate in my life—property better suited for the right person. How do you know who the right person is? For starters, nothing on the above list will apply to him. That's what it's like when he prioritizes you.

Think about it this way: You make time for things in your life that are a priority to you. You rearrange your schedule to spend time with your best friend; you get up at a certain time to make it to the gym before work; if someone needs a ride to the airport, you figure it out. All of those are priorities that you made a choice to order your life around. In the same way that you prioritize spending time with the guy you are dating, he should be doing the same for you. With the right guy, it's not a *should*. He *will*. On the flip side, if any of the above list resonated with you, there is a chance that *you* are the one treating *him* like an option. Don't do that to anyone.

God and Our Relationships

Despite all the questions I have about relationships, there has always been one thing I've never questioned: God wants to be involved in our relationships. All of them. Not when it's convenient, but all the time. God always has our best interests in mind. His plans for our lives are good, and I've learned that I'd rather do life with God instead of against him. Solomon, the author of Proverbs, reminds us that when we seek God, he will show us which direction to go (Prov. 3:5–6). This includes our relationships.

There is not a right or wrong way to allow God to be involved in your dating life. It doesn't look perfect, and it's not formulaic. But it's always helpful when you start by asking God what he thinks. Speaking for myself, when I develop a habit of regularly asking God about all areas of my life, it becomes second nature to also include the men I date. When I have a regular habit of reading God's Word, I am more inclined to be aware of when my actions or thought life start drifting in a direction that I don't want them to go. Inviting God into my relationships also looks like dating men who hold these same personal standards. So yes, I will always invite God into my relationships. I hope you do too.

The Worst Kind of Lonely

We may have convinced ourselves that being without anyone at all is the worst kind of lonely, but it's not. There is another type of lonely that is far worse—being with the wrong person. I interviewed a dozen or so married women on this subject, asking them to give just a few pieces of advice to those of us who are single. Do you know what most of them said? It's never worth it to settle for the *wrong person* just to have *a person*. No person is better than the wrong person. You don't want to put yourself in a position where you are fighting for someone who isn't interested in fighting for you.

When you discover that you're with the wrong person, how do you get out of it? It can be hard to psych yourself up to have that hard conversation. Dating is fun. Breakups are not. But moving away from the wrong person allows you to move toward the right person. Knowing this reminds you that ending the relationship with the wrong person is not the equivalent of ending the potential of a relationship with any person.

In the beginning stages of just messaging, when you discover this is the wrong person, politely respond and say, "No, thank you." Once you are more involved in the relationship and realize you need to get out, you don't need to continue to string him along. Recently a large group of my friends, both guys and girls, went on a weeklong beach vacation. There were a few dating couples on the trip. It was on the second day of the trip that one of the girls decided to end the relationship she was in. *Really?*

If you know this is no longer the right guy for you, end it prior to going on a trip like this—and certainly don't do it when there are still five more days of the vacation left! I realize most people won't find themselves in this specific situation, but the point is this: there are better and worse times to end a relationship. The better times are when the two of you are alone, not around a group of friends or at a crowded restaurant. Likewise, tell him over the phone or in person, not through a text.

Your Turn

When you know your worth, you stop giving other people discounts. I was having dinner with a friend recently and she was telling me about a guy that she met on an app about three months ago. The first month was great. They hit it off, went out a handful of times, and had a good time. The second month was more sporadic, but there were still a few good moments in there. Then there was this past month. He ghosted. He stopped replying to her text messages. As she was telling me this story, she had endured nearly three weeks of silence. She rationalized it as "he was busy." Then I heard the tone in her voice change. She began to talk herself into not being that interested in him after all. She knew it'd never work out. And while we were sitting there, he texted her. It was a Friday night. She replied instantaneously, launching into a text exchange for the next hour and a half. She didn't even recognize she was being treated as an option!

 When you know your worth, you stop giving other people discounts.

Women, we have the right to determine how we want to be treated. We have the right to say yes or to say no. If we don't want to be treated as an option, then we shouldn't allow it. To some extent, men will interact with us in the way that we interact with them. In the case of my friend, the guy was used to being able to show up when he pleased, so why would he think to do anything different in this instance? I believe that it doesn't take all of us, but it will take some of us, to change the situation. Some of us know we are valuable enough to be treated as a priority. The right guy will respond and rise to the occasion.

Questions for Reflection

1. Describe a time when you found yourself saying yes when you wanted to say no. Why do you think you said yes?
2. In what ways do women ignore warning signs in relationships? Have you done this? Why or why not?
3. Do you feel confident that you can say no to the guy who treats you like an option? Why or why not?
4. What does it look like for you to invite God into your relationships?

---[C H A P T E R   6]---

Options, Part 2: The Roster

We've been around rosters our entire lives. On the first day of
school, our teachers used the classroom roster to call our
names. (I'm sorry to those of you who have complicated first or last
names. One would think Kristin Fry is a pretty straightforward
name, but you'd be surprised at the variations people come up with.)
When we go to a sporting event, someone hands out a program with
a roster detailing the stats of all the players. If you have ever tried out
for a school team, you may remember waiting until the preassigned
time when the roster would be uploaded (or in my case, taped to
the inside of the classroom window), listing if you were in or out. It
was brutal, really. Though I suppose now with the everyone-gets-a-
trophy generation, when the roster goes up, everyone is automatically in. There still might be the chance that one coach will go rogue
and be bold enough to say, "No, I'm sorry you cannot be on this
team. This team is for varsity volleyball players. I'm sure you would
work really hard, but on this team, the ball needs to make it over the
net, not into it."

And then there's the dating roster. A dating roster is a tool that
many single folks use to keep themselves in the dating game without
having to really commit to anything serious. Rosters can be breeding
grounds for optionitis. But more than that, there is a danger that we
will treat them like a security blanket. Optionitis is a man's failure
to choose you, whereas your own roster reflects what you are doing
to men. Sometimes saying no means saying no to yourself and not

just the other person. A lot of single people use rosters to fill the gap between total loneliness and committed relationship.

You may be one of these people. A roster is filled with people you have connected with based on mutual interest, but neither of you have taken a step toward anything past flirting. A roster is what you pull out when you are questioning if anyone finds you attractive, interesting, or desirable. You only need to go through your list of previous matches to know that interested parties are in fact out there and all hope is not lost. Additionally, when things get rocky with your boyfriend, you may be tempted to pull out your roster and find security in knowing there is a plan B, should your current relationship go south.

I know a couple who had been dating exclusively for five months. But neither had made the decision to close out their dating apps. Occasionally when they were each home alone, they'd swipe through the profiles of various matches. It was fun. They figured it wasn't hurting anything to keep their options open and their roster current. Until they got matched with each other. Andy Stanley said it best when he said, "Finding real love requires an any-speed internet connection, but staying in love requires getting off the internet."[10] In this case it means: delete the dating apps. Delete the roster. My goal is to help you recognize your own roster and know when to delete it and why. When we eliminate the roster, we are essentially saying no to ourselves.

Women and Their Rosters

Women can spend weeks and even months flirting with guys—just from their roster. It's a way to fill your days and nights with all the attention you'll ever need; at least, that's what you've convinced yourself. Your roster spans the list of men wanting to have deep, intellectual, heartfelt conversations in a corner booth, to the guy who will take a selfie tour of town with you on a Saturday afternoon. The flirting seems innocent and no commitment is necessary, leaving you with what seems to be the best of both worlds. Validation with no strings attached, and the option to move on to someone new when you're bored.

Until one of two things happens. The first is this: you begin a new relationship. You like this guy. I mean, you *really* like this guy. Men from your roster pale in comparison. The second is far worse: your roster goes dark. Your week was busy and Friday couldn't come soon enough. After an exhausting five days, you check your phone— nothing. No texts, no calls, no comments, nothing. You panic. What about all those guys from your roster? You talk yourself off the ledge, trying to remind yourself that your worth is not found in the number of text messages received. You thought it was innocent flirting, but now that they've all gone radio silent, you realize that with every interaction you had allowed a deposit into your emotional bank account. Now you feel like everyone decided to withdraw the entire balance at the same time, leaving you bankrupt.

 If your goal is to marry a God-honoring, respectable man who will love and honor you, don't waste your time with a roster.

If your goal is to marry a God-honoring, respectable man who will love and honor you, don't waste your time with a roster. He won't be on it. Remember, as much as we think having a roster full of backups gives us a sense of feeling desired by men, it's a counterfeit fulfill- ment. I'm not saying that these men don't find you attractive, smart, or funny in the moment, but I am suggesting that because neither of you have taken a step toward any level of commitment—however minimal—it's fleeting. Besides, have you ever considered that when you say yes to a guy on your roster, you may be saying no to the guy you are really looking for?

Back to the first example. You are in a great relationship and things are going really well. But you still have a roster. There will come a point in the relationship where you have to make a decision: *Am I going to give this relationship the chance it deserves or not?* Only you can answer that question. Imagine if you were in the guy's position.

Together, you are having a serious conversation about the future of
your relationship. You are moving forward and are both on the same
page. Then you say to him, "I'm still going to keep my roster though.
You know, just in case." He would probably think, "Excuse me?"
How would that make him feel? I have to wonder if he'd even be willing to stay around after that. Let's say the roles were reversed. How
would you feel if the table was turned and he was saying that to *you*?
My guess is not too great. And if, by chance, you do think you'd be
totally fine with this scenario, then I'd question whether your current
relationship is the right, long-term fit.

Naturally, there could be fear attached to deleting your roster. What
are you going to do on Friday night when your Instagram feed reminds
you that the rest of the world is having fun while you are at home wondering why no one invited you? A roster sure would come in handy.

The Greatest Temptation

Deleting options and closing doors can be frightening, because we'll
never fully know what potential opportunities we turned down. But
it's just a reality of life: saying no will cost you something. Even though
we often wish it was free or easy, it's not. A lot of times, right decisions
are hard decisions and we have to give up something when we say no.
For example, saying no to a certain job that you know is not the right
fit may mean that you are giving up a higher paycheck or better ben-
efits. Saying no to a party may cost you an invite from that group of
friends ever again. Saying no to a particular relationship may cost you
companionship and someone to spend your Friday nights with. It will
be hard. That is, until we realize that we are giving up something we
like for the sake of keeping something we love. Say no to what's less
important so you can say yes to what's most important. For example,
say no to a list of people so you can say yes to one person.

Most of us need practice saying no. Sometimes we'll get it right and
sometimes we won't. That's okay. I also can't help but think about
someone who perfected the art of saying no. He lived the perfect balance of right now, wait, and not yet. And he unlocked the key to us
doing the same. Jesus lived the perfect human life. Not to flaunt it in

front of our face, but to teach us how to navigate life well. He taught us how to say no and why and when we need to say it.

Matthew was one of the twelve guys who had a front-row seat to the life and teachings of Jesus. Prior to this, he was a tax collector— meaning he wasn't exactly the most popular guy in town. Matthew received an invitation from Jesus to follow him. He did, and as far as we're told, Matthew never looked back. As part of this inner circle of the twelve who walked with Jesus, this disciple later went on to write an account of Jesus's life in what we know as the gospel of Matthew. It's the first book in the New Testament.

In his book, Matthew recorded one of the more profound moments of wisdom from Jesus's time on earth; it was a conversation between Jesus and his greatest adversary, Satan. Jesus had been fasting for forty days and forty nights. Afterward, he was led into the wilderness to be tempted. We read, "Then Jesus was led by the Spirit into the wilderness to be tempted by the devil. After fasting forty days and forty nights, he was hungry. The tempter came to him and said . . ." (Matt. 4:1–3).

Let me pause right here. When Matthew wrote "the tempter," he was talking about Satan, a created being who is the archenemy of God. Satan was trying to tempt Jesus to sin, and as we'll see, this wasn't some situation where God the Father was trying to see what Jesus was made of. Instead, Jesus modeled for us how to say no and overcome temptation, even in the face of our greatest wants. And Jesus empowers us to say no to what's good so we can say yes to what's great. Although Matthew recorded an interaction between Jesus and Satan, there are universal principles that apply to us today.

 Jesus empowers us to say no to what's good so we can say yes to what's great.

Have you ever been tempted by something you wanted? Maybe it was at work and your billable hours for the month fell just short of qualifying for that bonus you really needed. Isn't it tempting to just "find" a few more hours somewhere? Maybe HR didn't record all your vacation days from first quarter. It's tempting to not say anything because it would be nice to have a bit more time off in the summer. Or it's the new relationship, or the guy you've just met, or the three guys that you're chatting with offline, aside from your current relationship. It's tempting to say yes to all of them. Why? Because the alternative is to feel lonely and that doesn't sound very fun. The bottom line is that all of us can relate to temptation.

Back to the story: "The tempter came to him and said, 'If you are the Son of God, tell these stones to become bread'" (Matt. 4:3).

Jesus had just been fasting for forty days. That's a long time. And we are told he was hungry. Because I'm an endurance athlete, once I get past the two-hour mark of not having anything in my stomach, I'm about ready to eat a piece of paper. I'll eat just about anything. I can't imagine not having any food for forty days and forty nights. So, of course, the first thing that Jesus was tempted with was food. But it was more profound than mere food. Satan was tempting Jesus to meet his own needs. He was hungry, so no need to wait on anyone else, just go ahead and take care of that right now. Don't wait on the Father, do it yourself. Could Jesus turn those stones into bread? Absolutely. But what did he do instead? "Jesus answered, 'It is written: "Man shall not live on bread alone, but on every word that comes from the mouth of God"'" (Matt. 4:4).

In other words, Jesus said no. If he would have exercised his power to turn those stones into bread, he would have been acting independently of the Father. Jesus knew the dangers of allowing our circumstances to dictate our actions instead of acting according to God's best for our lives. We know what it's like to try to meet our own needs. Some of you have thought, "I've been single long enough and God hasn't brought the right guy, so I'm not waiting anymore. I'll just go date whoever I want, standards or not." When we do this, more often than not we end up in unhappy relationships. We may have compromised in ways we never expected to, or we have feelings of guilt or even loneliness because we're dating someone who we thought would meet our needs but he really doesn't. Meeting our own needs doesn't always lead to the happy ending we think it will.

The story with Jesus goes on. Instead of giving up, Satan tried again. (Temptation rarely goes away that easily.)

> Then the devil took him to the holy city and had him stand on the highest point of the temple. "If you are the Son of God," he said, "throw yourself down. For it is written:
> 'He will command his angels concerning you,
> and they will lift you up in their hands,
> so that you will not strike your foot against a stone.'"
> (Matt. 4:5–6)

In effect, Satan was saying to Jesus, "If you want to quote Scripture to me, then I'll quote it back to you." He challenged Jesus by saying if he was who he said he was, then he could throw himself off the temple and God would save him. Satan even used Scripture to prove it. However, Satan didn't get it right. In his challenge to Jesus, he purposefully omitted some crucial context. Had these verses been included, they would have stated that God protects those who are wholeheartedly following him, not those who merely want to put him to the test (Ps. 91). That's the trouble with temptation. It often mimics the right thing, and if we are not careful, we can convince ourselves that it's close enough. But again, Jesus said no: "Jesus answered him, 'It is also written: "Do not put the Lord your God to the test"'" (Matt. 4:7).

Satan tried one final time: "Again, the devil took him to a very high mountain and showed him all the kingdoms of the world and their splendor. 'All this I will give to you,' he said, 'if you will bow down and worship me'" (Matt. 4:8–9).

Here is the irony of Satan's temptation. After his death and resurrection, Jesus—who is God—received all power, authority, and dominion over heaven and earth. But the temptation was that he could have it all, and have it right then. Satan was offering a shortcut. "Bypass the cross and all its suffering, and this can be yours," Satan was telling him. The catch behind the devil's offer? Sell your soul. Isn't that the way it works with us too? We can wait for the right guy for our happily ever after, or we can give in to the temptation of the guy right in front of us. He might not give us what we are ultimately looking for in a relationship, but he'll definitely fill the void in the meantime. Is that worth it?

Matthew concluded the story:

> Jesus said to him, "Away from me, Satan! For it is written: 'Worship the Lord your God, and serve him only.'"
> Then then devil left him, and angels came and attended him. (Matt. 4:10–11)

Jesus said no again and finally, the tempter left. Three types of temptations. Three times Jesus said no. To put it simply, Satan tempted Jesus with the immediate pleasures of life, tempted him to prove himself, and tempted him with all the possessions he could possibly want. Why did Jesus say no to all those things? Why should we say no to all those things, especially when they are within arm's reach?

It is so easy to say yes to the guy who isn't the best fit for us when he is in front of us, right there on our roster. He is interested and available, so what's the harm? Or, there is the guy with the steady income and increasing upward mobility, with a future promising all the luxuries in a life you have only dreamed about. But he doesn't treat you right. That's why he's just a backup on your roster. He's a good time, a temporary solution. Why should we say no? The reason is simpler than you think. Saying no to what's less important allows you to say yes to what's most important.

Jesus modeled this for us. If you were to continue in the book of Matthew, you would read that after the temptation with Satan, Jesus began his public preaching ministry. It was after saying no to temptation that Jesus was then able to begin his public ministry of teaching the message of salvation. If Jesus had said yes to any one of the three temptations that Satan offered, he would have been saying no to the cross, to the resurrection, and to bridging the gap between all of humankind and God the Father. There would be no personal relationship with God. Jesus would have been saying no to the plan that was set in motion since the fall in the garden of Eden, a plan that would allow people to put their hope in a Savior and have eternal life. But he didn't do that. Instead, Jesus chose to say no to what seemed good at the time, knowing that he was saying yes to what was best for the future.

Your Best No

My friend Gerald has taught me a lot about what it looks like to say no to yourself. He and I cohosted a quarterly event for several years running. It was an evening of teaching and worship for two thousand–plus Atlanta-area singles who were involved in North Point Ministries. When I say cohost, what I really mean is that I tried to give helpful information while Gerald made fun of me. Each night, we'd be backstage and he'd convince me that this was going to be the night he would find a husband for me.

However, his version of finding me a husband typically involved pimping me onstage to a room full of hundreds of eligible bachelors. One night, we were promoting the summer social gatherings and Gerald interjected, while onstage mind you: "Who wants to sign up for a gathering to date Kristin?" (He's like the little brother I never wanted.) The irony of it all, though, is that one of those first nights we hosted together is the very night he met his future wife. I guess his charades worked for one of us. Despite the jokes, he's a great friend and a wonderful communicator.

I bring up Gerald because he taught on the temptation of Jesus one night in this room full of single adults. He summed it up brilliantly. He said, "Jesus said no to get where he ultimately wanted to go."[11] Jesus had a picture in mind for his future. When you know where you're going, it's easier to say no to the things that will prevent you from getting there.

The application is twofold. I asked a handful of single men and women if they thought anyone on their roster represented marriage material. Do you know what all of them said without hesitation?

Nope. None of the men and women would marry anyone on their roster. If you find yourself in that same category, then my advice to you is to clear it.

The second point is more important, so please don't miss this. Social media and dating apps have given us a false sense of perfection. What do I mean by that? When we are scrolling through someone's profile or our social media feeds for a potential match, we are only looking at the highlight reel. We all know this. The effect, however, is that it plays a mind game and we begin thinking their life must be perfect, which can cause us to question our own life. We wonder why we are not living this perfect life that everyone else seems to have.

Specifically, when we are in a relationship with someone and we are at the crossroads of decision-making, wondering if we should delete the roster and go all in, this false sense of perfection can trip us up. When we see someone else's relationships on social media, we are only seeing the best parts. But to us, it looks perfect. We can falsely believe that there is a perfect decision when it comes to who we are dating.

The truth is that there is no perfect relationship and no perfect person. There is a perfect person for us, but that's different than being independently perfect. Similarly, there is more than one perfect person for us. Too many times, I see both men and women say no to matches because they are holding out for "the one." You know, the imaginary soul mate. But "the one" is the person that you choose. When you say I do, that person has now become "the one." Can you imagine how difficult it would be if—out of 7.5 billion people—God only designed everyone to be matched with just one person? And your job was to relentlessly search the globe, trying to locate that person? What if you couldn't find him or her? Does that mean there is no hope of you ever getting married? Of course not. That would be silly. It would also be rather mean of God, and God doesn't operate like that.

If we are not careful, we will allow ourselves to become fearful that we might make an imperfect decision, or a wrong decision. This has the potential to lead us to not make any decision at all. The outcome?

We remain in a perpetual state of limbo within our current relationship and with those we consider as backups. No one will win in that situation.

Currently, I'm typing this chapter on my MacBook. For those of you who are Mac users, you know that you can allow your text messages to come across the top of your computer screen. While I was typing this chapter, a text message from a dear friend came across the top corner. It read, "I'm so over being single." I laughed out loud at the irony of the timing, of course. And then I had to tell her. It reminded me that being single has a unique set of challenges. It can be lonely and overwhelming, and cause us to doubt God's goodness in his plan for us and simply throw in the towel. But when we have our best yes in mind, I firmly believe that God will honor our noes. That's what Jesus taught us to do.

Questions for Reflection

1. What would it look like to say no to yourself, thus saying no to your roster? What's holding you back?
2. Do you agree that by keeping a roster, you are treating the men on that roster unfairly? Why or why not?
3. Describe a time when you found yourself thinking that someone else was in a perfect relationship. How did you feel?
4. Do you believe that there is not just one person for you? Why or why not?

─────────────[C H A P T E R   7]─────────────

Friends You Want to Have

Most of us have probably had family experiences that left us won-dering why we weren't born into another set of relational dynam-ics. I know I have. For the past two decades, I've been trying to get my family to admit I was adopted because—in my mind—that was the only logical explanation for our stark differences. Besides, that would free me up from having to claim any of their embarrassing behaviors as a personal reflection on me. However, given the fact that I am a mirror image of a perfect combination of both of my parents . . . well, it has left me with no other option but to claim their genetics as mine.

Can you relate? Last year, just before Thanksgiving, I chatted with a friend about her plans for the holiday. She and her parents were taking a road trip to spend the day with extended family members. It would just be the three of them traveling: my friend, her mom, and her dad. Or, so she thought. Right before our conversation, her father had called to tell her to pack light. That seemed odd. They would only be making an overnight journey, and in her parents' SUV to boot. Then her father informed her that the family pets were going too. That meant she would be crammed into the middle of the back seat, wedged between the cat's litter box and the dog's car seat. While Fido would be buckled in to her right, the cat would roam free, most likely to make laps around the interior of the car for all six hours of the drive. Not to mention a repeat performance on the return trip. Like me, she was beginning to question her genetics.

But, let's face it: you don't get to choose your family. That's an undisputed fact. For some of you, if given the chance, you'd choose

them anyway. That is something I hope you never take for granted. Families form some of the most powerful bonds between individuals on this earth. However, others of you may wish you were born into a different set of circumstances. I can understand that. But if that's you, here's the good news: you do get to choose your friends. Whether good family or bad, there is something special that happens when you form relationships based on choice.

Think about it this way. We all know that the fourth Thursday in November is Thanksgiving. (In the event you were wondering how that happened, you can thank Congress.) Most people in America spend Thanksgiving with both immediate and extended family members. There is a reason the day before Thanksgiving is the most traveled day of the year in the United States. Thanksgiving is one of those obligatory holidays that people generally don't pass on.

For single folks, though, there is another unofficial holiday that has been growing with increasing popularity. Friendsgiving. It's a way to celebrate the holiday with the "family" of your choosing. Friendsgiving is one of those rare holidays without family baggage, relational tensions, and relatives you fear might expire right there on the couch, due to age or overconsumption of adult beverages. It's an evening where friends gather together to give thanks on their own terms. It's typically a potluck-style meal in a judgment-free zone. The best part? Celebrating with only people you like, only food you like, and only for as long as you like, forever and ever, amen. My guess is that most of you reading this book have taken part in your own Friendsgiving.

God did not create us to do life alone. Whether introverted or extroverted, most of us don't need convincing of that. We are wired to connect with people. It makes our lives more fun and less lonely. It's the reason we make up holidays to celebrate these connections and commonalities. We like to attach ourselves to whatever community we belong to, or want to join. It's one of the reasons we all wear the same colors of our favorite team. Whenever I move to a new city, I always buy a hat with that city's football team's logo. Call me a bandwagon fan if you want, but I am unashamedly proud of all the teams I've adopted as my own over the years.

If you have ever lived in the South, by the way, then you know just how extreme people take this when it comes to college football. I mean, SEC and ACC football fans are no joke. I'm fairly confident that people end up in each other's wills solely based on which college football team they pledged allegiance to. I mean that in all the best ways, though I'm sure some might disagree.

When you don't have people to connect to, you feel it. For example, if you've ever moved to a new city or state in your post-college years, you know how challenging it can be to start over. For the first weeks or even months in your new hometown, my guess is that you spent a lot of time alone. You may have even been on a first-name basis with the employees of all the fast food restaurants within a two-mile radius. At least that's how it was for me. Besides the fact that I spent the first six months using my phone's GPS to get home every single day, I was desperate for a friend. Just one.

It didn't seem like too big of a request. I wanted someone to go for a walk with, see a movie together, get a burger (so I didn't have to bring a book or my laptop to the restaurant and pretend like I was working and meant to be alone), and have conversations about nothing and everything, all at the same time. I felt incredibly disconnected. But eventually the pieces came together, and I built my community. It took work, however—and intentionality. Good, deep, meaningful friendships don't just fall out of the sky. But I knew how important it was, so I was committed to putting in the work.

 There is this misconception that once you get into a dating relationship, you don't need friends.

Unfortunately, there is this misconception that once you get into a dating relationship, you don't need friends. That's why this is such an important chapter. I have a hard time finding any evidence in Scripture that points to this. I'm pretty sure God never said, "Thou shalt not need friends once thou art married." I've also had several conversations with my married girlfriends about whether their husbands are a sufficient substitute for girlfriends. The resounding answer is, "No." Case in point: they have not ended their friendships with me and have assured me that is not in their plans.

Too many times I've seen people get into relationships, ditch their friends, end the dating relationship, and then come back to their friends—only to realize their friendships are not the same as before. Besides, your friends will feel used if you do this to them. The unfortunate reality is that some of them may not be as willing to pick the friendship back up once you've decided they're convenient again. I realize that may sound harsh to some, but trust me, I've seen this happen too many times to count. So, I'd rather tell you on the front end as a preventative measure.

If you think that a boyfriend will end any desire for other friendships, I'd strongly encourage you to consider that there may be an alternative way of thinking. Friendships are important whether you're single, dating, or married. Not just any friendships, but intentional, life-giving, community-building friendships. And that's what we're going to talk about. What do those friendships look like, why are they important, and how do you find them?

One Another

I have found that being connected to other people, whether we're single or in a relationship, is important to God too. In fact, it's so important that God has even provided a list of "to-dos" in interacting with people in relationship. Now, it's not a to-do list like the checklist your parents gave you to finish your chores. Or the ones you've made for yourself because you are a type A personality and checking things off your list is more important than the act of completing the task. Think of it more like a list of incredibly helpful suggestions that—like Andy Stanley says—when you do them will not only make your life better but will also make you better at life.[12] But really though, as a Christ follower, these are not so much things we are *supposed to do* as they are things that we *want to do*, because that's what happens when we grow in our relationship with God. God has put these to-dos in the form of "one anothers."

Did you know that in the New Testament of the Bible, there are fifty-nine "one-another" statements? Fifty-nine times we are told to love one another, forgive one another, encourage one another, or follow some other form of one-another. Anything that gets repeated with that level of frequency? It's worth paying attention. I have found that when God tells us to do something, the motivation is always with our best interests in mind. He knows it will make our life better.

In the second half of the book of Hebrews in the New Testament, the writer is speaking to Christians, encouraging them to not give up meeting together (10:23–25). The author gave this charge because Christians were falling prey to the competing worldview at the time. Sound familiar? How many times have you been influenced by the differing opinions around you? I know I have. But the author knew that if the Christians continued to meet with one another and encourage one another, they would also be able to continually point one another toward what was true and good, as opposed to the lies and confusing messages that we are so apt to believe when we fade into isolation.

But you need real, true, intentional girlfriends for this to happen. While we are told to not give up meeting with one another, we are also told to encourage one another, be happy with those who are happy, be sad alongside those who are sad, speak truth to one another, and pray for one another. For me, I cannot imagine a life without the friends I can do this with. Well, I can imagine it—and it sounds really lonely.

It's our friends who are able to cheer for us when a great guy comes into our lives. They're the ones who listen to all the uninteresting-to-anyone-else details of our first conversations with a new guy, and they enjoy every minute of it. And because we've developed honest and safe friendships, when our emotions cloud our judgment and things start sounding fishy, it's our friends who will share the hard truth with us. That's the way it's supposed to be. God has told us to love one another, and loving one another means being truthful with one another. So when I say that the one-anothers in the Bible are more than just a checklist, I mean it. They really do make your life better. I've experienced it and I want that experience for you too.

Several years ago, Andy was doing a sermon series at North Point Community Church about various bad church experiences. He closed the series with an attention-grabbing statement in his case for community. He said the primary activity of the church was one-anothering one another.[13] If that's the primary activity of the church, then by default that's our primary activity too. It's my job and your job. There's no way around that. In case there was any confusion, it's incredibly difficult for these one-anothers to happen if we are not connected to each other in relationship. I didn't say impossible, just difficult. But if you're always trying to one-another a stranger, you're probably missing the point. That's why we need friends. Real friends.

Depth, Not Breadth

So how do you put the one-anothers into action and build deep, meaningful friendships? For a lot of us, we end up moving away from our families, which results in us not seeing them on a daily basis. But our friends are a different story. As adults, friends are the ones who typically do daily life with us. They come to our house, know where we work, and may have even met a few of our coworkers. Our friends are the ones who pass our crazy neighbor when they come to visit us and would probably notice if we didn't show up somewhere that we'd typically be. When you don't live geographically near your family, these are not things your family would notice.

You need to create a friend family. Be intentional about surrounding yourself with close friends. You don't need a lot, but you do need some. What is a friend family? They are the types of friends where you can speak words without context, editing, or disclaimers, because these friendships are authentic, raw, and vulnerable. Everyone needs to have these types of friends in their life.

How do you know if you have these friendships? Here are some indicators:

- You don't need to filter your words for fear of rejection or fear that your friend might think differently about you.
- You don't need to constantly justify what you said or what you did. Your friend gets it, and more importantly, your friend knows you.
- When all hell breaks loose in your life (and it's inevitable that at some point it will), you have someone to call. Not only will they actually pick up the phone, they will also drive over to your house. Probably with chocolate.
- When it's two in the morning and your house floods, your delayed flight lands at the airport, or you lock your keys in the car, you have a friend who will help.
- You're not afraid to cry in front of them.
- They make sure you're not alone on major holidays (unless, of course, you want to be).
- You're not afraid to apologize to them, and they're not afraid to forgive you.

If you can't relate to any of these things on this list, it may be worth reevaluating the friendships in your life. But, it's not too late. It's never too late to cultivate real friendships. Yes, it will take time, risk, and vulnerability. But you'll never regret it.

Friendships like this don't happen overnight and not all friendships will be like this, but some will. Everybody needs some body, preferably some bodies. Meaningful friendships all have two things in common: transparency and consistency. There is a regular frequency of interaction. Over time, you are increasingly transparent with what you're thinking and feeling. If you don't have people in your life you see regularly, then find them and commit to a regular time. If you need to join a consistent community group or Bible study, then do it. Friends won't happen unless you decide that you want them to and make the effort.

It may be at this point that you're thinking, "Those types of friendships sound awesome, but how do I find them?" Let me give you an example of what I observed recently with a small group of twentysomethings that I led. I have been leading small groups for over twenty years now, and a few years back I decided to start a brand-new group with twenty-two- and twenty-three-year-olds. They signed up for my group through church. Before I knew it, I had fourteen girls who, for the most part, were complete strangers sitting in a circle. At least half of them were brand-new to town and knew no one. But somewhere along the way, these girls had learned that being an adult meant learning to take initiative in developing friends. That's exactly what they did. Every week these girls showed up for our small group.

The first month of conversations was more lighthearted, easing into transparency over time. It mimicked small talk more than full disclosure. But during our first meeting, I looked at them and said what I say whenever I start a new group: "You are all sitting in a circle, sizing each other up in your minds, wondering if you could actually be friends with her. I get that. But I'm going to ask that you give it four weeks until you decide whether or not you like these people and whether or not you want to be in this group. A lot can happen in four weeks if you're willing to at least give it that much. Besides, a lot of you have figured out how to make bad relationships work for far longer than that, so you can stick this out."

They all laughed—awkwardly, but they stayed, and an incredible thing happened. These girls intentionally showed up to grow in friendships and listened to each other talk about their lives. Those first impressions from night one became a distant memory as they forged real impressions over time—as a result of sharing honest details about their lives. The reason they were able to be honest was because of their predictability in showing up week after week. It was a group that proved trustworthy; when people are trustworthy, we feel safe. Feeling safe is the breeding ground for real, lasting friendships. With this group of girls, several went on to become roommates, others became bridesmaids, and the friendships have exceeded far beyond one night a week.

My encouragement to you is this: friendships like this will happen, as long as you are willing to put in the time. Your church might not do small groups, but there may be another event to attend. For me, whenever I move to a new town, I ask everyone I know for connections in my new city, and then I call strangers, asking them if we can meet up. I tell them I'm new and am looking to meet some people. I have never been turned down, and my guess is that you probably won't be either. Some of those strangers are now my best friends.

Proximity Does Not Equal Intimacy

In contrast to these deep friendships, digital friendships can be deceptively superficial. There is an abundance of social media networking tools designed to make us feel connected. Yet, too many of us feel alone and isolated. Why? Because being virtually connected is counterfeit intimacy. It's fake. Seeing a highlight reel from your vacation on Facebook, or watching weekend snaps uploaded to your Insta story, does not automatically produce a deeply connected friendship. I can see either of those things equally as well from a stranger who friended me after a speaking engagement as I can from my BFF. So can you.

Now, I'm not arguing that social networking is bad. In fact, I love it. Besides, that would be counterproductive to the point of this book. I am arguing, though, not to confuse your Facebook friends with your real ones. Unless you can cite all your Facebook friends' first and last names, including the city in which you first met them in person, then I'd be willing to let you slide. Yeah, me neither.

What's on the Other Side of Me?

Another important reason you need connections that go deeper than likes and filtered photos is that close friends will shoot straight with you. Even when it doesn't necessarily feel great. We've already talked about this, but my reason for bringing it up again is this reality: Whatever habits, baggage, or relational patterns you have now will not magically go away when you start dating someone. Who you are before you date someone is who you are when you date someone. This even includes the things you said you'd stop doing once you got into a new relationship: "Next time I'll stand up for myself," or "Next time I won't walk into this new relationship distrustful just because the last guy cheated on me." The only way you will be fully aware of whether you are behaving in ways that are unproductive and unhelpful is if (1) you are in real community with friends who have experienced these behaviors from you and (2) you invite your friends to be honest with you.

 Who you are before you date someone is who you are when you date someone.

Good friends love you from the inside out but see you from the outside in. We can't see ourselves from the outside in, but good friends can serve as a mirror. They love us just the way we are but are not afraid to tell us the hard truths. If they are afraid to tell you, then maybe you need to give them permission. A friend of mine, Jeff Henderson, who worked with me at North Point Ministries, is one of the best models of giving people permission to speak openly into his life. He taught me to do the same. He challenged several of us with the task of finding at least three people and asking them the question, "What's it like to be on the other side of me?"

Now the trick is to ask people outside of your mom who, for some of you, already thinks you're the smartest, most beautiful, perfect-in-every-way daughter. Her feedback might not be what's most helpful. The other piece to this exercise is to ask people who know you well. In other words, asking your cube-mate at work who rarely interacts with you will not provide you with helpful information—outside of whether you talk too loudly on your phone. Ask people who know you in more than one area of life and have a perspective that you value. You can gather this information in a few different ways: You can send out an email or create a survey for people to give their feedback anonymously. For the really thick-skinned, you can set up several coffee dates and ask them in an honest, face-to-face conversation.

Here's the moral of the story. It's worth gathering this information from trusted friends now because if your friends experience something from you, then most certainly the person you're going to date will experience it from you too. I assure you, it is much easier to develop self-awareness and course-correct now while you're single than it is while you're trying to manage your own personality, life experiences, and habits, along with the person you're dating and everything he brings to the table. Like my counselor once told me, "Kristin, you may as well unpack your [emotional] bag now because if you don't, you'll end up needing a bigger suitcase for yours and his once you start getting serious." Your baggage doesn't go away once you start dating someone, and you're the only one who can do the unpacking. So if you're not planning on buying a bigger suitcase, I'd go ahead and start unpacking now, with your friends' help.

Ground Rules

Let's talk specifics as friendships relate to dating. Not only will your friends be your biggest advocates, encouragers, and truth-tellers, they will also provide something else that is basic to every new dating relationship: safety. Listen, before you roll your eyes, this is serious. I understand that dating apps are the wave of the current century and that everybody's doing it. With that said, you may feel there is no cause for alarm. But that's not what I'm arguing. I'm not trying to go down the route of the overprotective parent who doesn't realize you are twentysomething years old and have managed to make sound decisions thus far concerning your well-being, and can therefore make a few good decisions about who and how you date. Trust me, I get it. That would be annoying if I were that person. But hear me out on this one. I am arguing that none of the above is an excuse to not take a little precaution.

Here are some basic, commonsense dating app ground rules.

1. *Tell someone the details of your first date.* When you make an arrangement via a dating app to meet up in person, please tell someone. Whether you've already graduated to texting and phone calls, or it was a last-minute decision with a match you made during your lunch break that day, tell someone. Text at least one friend and tell them

(1) who you are meeting, (2) what time you are meeting him, and (3) where you are going. This may seem like overkill, but remember, this is still someone you've never met. You have no context for how he acts in a social setting, around peers, or around you. You know that you're attracted to his photos, you're intrigued by his profile, and you've enjoyed his virtual flirting. All of that led to an in-person meeting. *But he is still a stranger.*

My roommate always told me when she was going out on a first date. Now granted, we are in our thirties, so I didn't expect her to necessarily walk back in the door by ten o'clock after a Friday night date. But if it started pushing one in the morning, you better believe I was going to send off an "are you alive?" text before heading to sleep myself.

Here is the added benefit: it feels good knowing that someone is looking out for you. If you're having a great date and lose track of time, and a text comes through from your friend, do you know what that means? It means that someone values you and cares about you, and you are worth their time to be sure you're okay. It feels really good on the receiving end of that text and to be reminded that you matter. Because you know what? You do. So go ahead and do yourself a favor and let a friend know where you are going and who you are going with.

2. *Make a plan to have an out if the date is not going well.* It's an easy thing to do and prevents you from getting stuck in a bad situation. I have had multiple friends over the past few years who always do this. They tell me when and where they are going on a date, and ask me to text either sixty or ninety minutes in. The time depends on whether they are meeting him for coffee or for dinner. My text is always the same: "Hey, can you call me?" If the date is going poorly, they will call me back and then apologize to the guy for needing to leave. If the date is going well, my friend will simply reply with, "I'll text you later." And then I know that everyone is okay.

Fortunately, I've only found myself on a painful first date a few times. But had I put this simple tip into practice sooner, those are hours I could have avoided wasting. I do know for a fact, though, that my current roommate appreciates the texts and there have been multiple times where she wished the text came sooner. Still, she was more than thankful when it finally flashed across her screen. She desperately needed an out. And you may too.

3. *Tell someone when you get home.* It's one thing to let your friends know where and when you're going out, but follow-up is key. I'm not asking for a tell-all at midnight, just a quick: "I made it home; I'll talk to you tomorrow." We'll all sleep easier at night if you do this. I also know plenty of girls who will run out to meet a match over lunch or an afternoon cup of coffee during the work week. Same rules apply here. If you don't have that kind of relationship with coworkers, shoot a friend a text and let them know you made it back to your desk.

Galentine's Day

It's never too late to form deeply committed friendships, and it can be one of the more important decisions you make in your life. From personal experience, I can say with 100 percent confidence that life is better connected to people. You can't choose your family, and you don't always get to choose your coworkers or neighbors, but you can choose your friends. Choose the friends you want to be around, the ones whose lives you want to emulate, the ones who bring out the best in you, and make the decision to spend lots of time with them. Besides, thanks to the sitcom *Parks and Recreation*, we all now have another way to spend Valentine's Day when we find ourselves dateless: Galentine's Day. You're definitely going to need those gal-friends if or when that day rolls around.

Questions for Reflection

1. Who are the friends in your life? Are they the type of friends you can call at all hours of the day about anything? Why or why not?
2. If you don't have the friends you want to have, what is one change you can make to begin to develop some? If you do have the friends you want to have, what is one change you could make to make your friendships even stronger?

3. Have you ever ditched your friends once you began a new dating relationship? What was the effect on your friendships?
4. Have you ever found yourself in a dating situation where you wished you had a plan for a way out? Is there a plan you can put in place with a friend for future dates?

Relationships Worth Waiting For

While they are fun to watch, romantic comedies have given us false ideals when it comes to what good, healthy relationships look like. Don't get me wrong, I've probably watched them all. Because, deep down, I'm a bit of a hopeless romantic. On some level, maybe we all are, but not everyone will own up to it. For me, it's why I always root for the last woman standing on *The Bachelor*. My friends make fun of me for it, reminding me that those relationships are not birthed from reality. Yes, I do realize this. But every season I have hope that it will work *this time*. We all know it usually doesn't because a foundation of substance is typically required for building anything of value. Four money-is-no-object dates over an eight-week period, leading to a proposal on one knee, doesn't usually classify as substance. Or reality. I still want it to work though!

Romantic comedies can be even more misleading. You don't always meet the man of your dreams by accidentally spilling your coffee on a total stranger (who happens to be incredibly attractive) at Starbucks while rushing out the door to work. But when you lock eyes after apologizing profusely, you know it's forever. However, you forgot to exchange phone numbers—or names. The good news is that you miraculously run into him the next day at the dog park. He asks you out and it's pure bliss. Until one of you cheats on the other. But there's more: It was all a big misunderstanding. Somehow, with three and a half minutes remaining in the movie, he chases you down, reciting the most romantic monologue since Shakespeare, and you realize you made a mistake by cutting him loose. The two of you are reunited and he becomes the man to set the bar for all other men to come after him. You both live happily ever after together with your dog and 1.84 kids in a great neighborhood with matching cars. After crying from a roller coaster of emotions during the final act of the movie, I believe that women still silently whisper to God, asking him for that to be their love story too. I know I used to do that.

That's not reality! Yet we subconsciously hold on to these story lines as ideal, secretly hoping they'll become our own personal fairy tale. For starters, we have dating apps. Lots of them. We are on lots of them. Unless you want to say it's love at first swipe. Which I suspect we will begin to hear more and more.

The point is that romantic comedies don't always give us an accurate depiction of healthy relationships. Still, we are tempted to hold these fictitious characters as the standard for our lives. While we all may hope for the *Pretty Woman* ending, the man of our dreams is probably not going to ride up to our bedroom window on a white horse. In broad daylight. On the city streets of Los Angeles. For starters, you can't just go and rent a white horse. Secondly, in this day and age someone would probably steal the horse before the guy even made it to you. So what is the standard for relationships? What does God have to say about healthy relationships? What does that look like in action? How will we recognize a relationship worth waiting for, or rather, the man worth waiting for? The right man. As a disclaimer, the right man can absolutely be just one swipe away. Charlie Puth may need to rewrite his song "See You Again."

The Golden Rule

Even if the right man is just one swipe away, relationships don't move forward without common ground and mutual respect. Enter the Golden Rule: Do unto others as you would have them do unto you. You probably learned it in kindergarten. I have a vague recollection of the Golden Rule written in yellow on one of the walls in my classroom. To be honest, I may have slightly understood it when I was younger, but I certainly didn't care to apply it until later in life.

Growing up, I was more focused on getting even than being nice.

Kids can be cruel. I wasn't about to let them get away with that. I'm still trying to recover from the time I was six years old and some of the older kids threw my stuffed animal out the window on the bus ride home. I know what you're thinking. No, I was not in the habit of bringing stuffed animals to school, but I was only six. It was show-and-tell day and that was my show-and-tell of choice. I'm certain that day set the stage on some subconscious level for me wanting to pay back evil for evil throughout the rest of my elementary and middle school years. That's probably not what the Golden Rule had in mind.

The Golden Rule is the basic law of reciprocity. I wouldn't have been such a mean kid had I taken this to heart in elementary school. But in the early days, the only thing I cared about was someone feeling the same hurt that I did. I told someone just last night that if I didn't have a personal relationship with God, and if it didn't matter so much to me now that I was living my life in a way that honored Jesus, then I would absolutely be a mean girl. You know the movie. A 2004 classic. Thankfully God is in the business of transforming us from the inside out. About a year ago, I was telling a friend about how I wish I was little bit nicer to people. His reply? "Kristin, you're one of the nicest people I've ever met." I about fell out of my chair. If that is not a testament to God's redemption of character, I'm not sure what is.

The Ultimate Standard

Whether in the context of dating or friendship, work or family, Jesus set the standard for the ultimate "Golden Rule." When Jesus walked the earth, the Pharisees were a religious group who strictly followed the Jewish law (or at least claimed they did). They opposed Jesus because they believed that Jesus was opposing their laws. These guys were the ultimate rule followers—and hypocrites.

The Pharisees knew the law backward and forward, but there were a lot of laws and they were hard to keep. There were 613 commandments in the law, divided into 248 positive ones and 365 negative ones. All joking aside, can you imagine if we had to order our daily lives around that many commandments? It would be hard to have any normal or lighthearted interactions with anyone. The only filter you would know how to see the world through is: "Am I getting this right?"

One particularly well-versed Pharisee came to Jesus and asked him about the greatest commandment in the law. Most people believe this was a sincere question. Put yourself in the shoes of this Pharisee. There are a lot of laws, and if one was more important than the others, I'd probably want to know too. You may remember how Jesus answered: "'Love the Lord your God with all your heart and with all your soul and with all your mind.' . . . And the second is like it: 'Love your neighbor as yourself'" (Matt. 22:37, 39).

Jesus didn't compare the commandments or lay down some mechanical rule in his reply. Instead, he said that above all else our motivation should first and foremost be to love God with every part of our being. It's more than just good feelings toward God; it's about the will as well as the heart. When we love God first, then we will more naturally be inclined to do things motivated by our love instead of by our own selfish ambitions.

Think about it like this. Most of you probably have someone in your life that you love. It may be a family member, or someone else. Even when they make you mad, deep down you still love them. If you were to get an emergency phone call about one of them, either during work hours or in the middle of the night, my guess is that you'd drop everything, walk out the door, and show up. Why? Because you love them, not because you're *supposed to* care. That's how God wants it to work with us. Which is why he gives us the second greatest commandment in his response as well. When you love God first, everything he tells us after that is easy. Love your neighbor as yourself. Of course, this is not your literal neighbor, although that person is included too. Your neighbor is any person besides you. It's everyone. Jesus's words mean that you should treat people the way you want to be treated, including those you date. That's powerful.

What does it look like to love God in your everyday life—and then go and love people like that? For both you and the guy you date, it looks like taking care of your relationship with God first, before you take care of the relationship with the other person. In other words, spending time alone with God in Scripture or in prayer is still a priority. Loving God means desiring a growing relationship with him. Not a relationship when it's convenient for you or when you have nothing else to do. You actively want to know what God says about you, about him, and about life. Loving God also means that your actions line up with the principles God has set. It's one thing to know what God says about treating people, but loving God and then loving other people means that we will actually follow through and treat them that way.

 Treat people the way you want to be treated, including those you date.

God's Golden Rule isn't just about loving others. It helps us recognize how we are supposed to be loved and treated by others. The right man will want to love you like this. The right man will follow the Golden Rule as Jesus defined it. To love you in the way he wants to be loved. The right man will have a deep love for God that will lead him to a natural overflow of loving others well—loving others well as God defines it. That includes you. Treating you with honor and respect will be a no-brainer to him. The right man won't have to force himself to do it. His love will motivate him to. That's a relationship worth waiting for. Women want to feel safe and cared for in a relationship. Men want to feel respected. It may not look like a Disney movie, but I can guarantee you that it's possible. The reason that it's possible is because that is how God transforms us and our relationships when we love him. Imagine if you had a relationship like that. Wouldn't it be worth waiting for?

Real Time

What does God's kind of love look like in a day-to-day relationship? Luckily, a lot of us have friends who are in marriages we hope to emulate. I do. I feel so fortunate to have friends around me who have shown me what's possible for my own life, both in a dating relationship and in a marriage worth waiting for. I might add that some of them met their spouse on a dating app. There's hope. Great men use dating apps.

So, rather than continue with the theoretical, I thought I'd share some of their real-life accounts. I sat down with over thirty married couples, any one of whom I'd love to have a marriage like theirs. They shared the qualities in the other person that stole their hearts while dating, and they talked about the key to keeping their marriages both fun and healthy. Now granted, a lot of you, like me, have probably dated men who had wonderful qualities. So it's not as though we have never seen what a man of quality looks like. But speaking for myself, when the relationship falls apart, I find myself wondering if the right guy is really still out there. These accounts from men and women I respect remind me that he exists.

In the numerous conversations I had, several themes rose to the top. They were repeated over and over again by both males and females. For simplicity, I broke them into categories. Here are the things that were most repeated as key to a great relationship.

1. *"We" before "me" or "you."* Nearly every couple talked about seeing themselves on the same team. I think most of us can relate to what that would be like. Whether it's a dance team, kickball team, work team, board of directors, or community service team, we all know that being on a team means that we put the good of the team before our own self-interests. The answer becomes what's best for us, not what's best for me. Now this doesn't mean there will never be times of disagreement. Not one couple stated that they agreed on everything, every time. A healthy relationship is not void of fighting, conflict, or misunderstanding. A healthy relationship commits to resolution. Couples learn to fight fair. Fighting fair means that you don't argue just to prove a point; it means you engage in dialogue that will allow each person to feel heard and understood. This results in an agreed-upon resolution extending beyond one person being right and feeling justified. Instead, you seek to understand over being right. That's what you do when you're a team.

There have been times when I have gotten angry with the person I was dating. I was hurt and I wanted him to know he was responsible for that hurt. In those moments, I remember thinking that I had a choice to make. I could choose to be angry and either give him the silent treatment for who knows how long, or speak words so cutting he'd be forced to agree with me or walk away entirely. Or I could choose to let my emotions calm down and have a neutral conversation, putting myself in his shoes to try and understand why he said or did the things he did. I chose the latter because "we" was better than "me." I did not dismiss my feelings or deny that I was hurt, but I sought to understand his perspective in addition to my own. When you are in a relationship, you are not the only one with feelings and experiences to take into consideration. Trying to prove a point just because it's good for me isn't always what is ultimately good for us. To sum it up in one word: compromise. People in a healthy relationship understand this, and it's key to being a great team.

2. *I'm sorry.* You're not always right. You don't always have to be right. It's okay to admit both of those things. Women in particular noted how much they love that their husbands are not afraid to admit when they are wrong and apologize for it. Equally, it has challenged the women to readily admit when they are wrong as well. It takes a certain level of humility to admit that you don't always have it all together. Jesus displayed the ultimate form of humility as an example for us (Phil. 2:4–11). Men who love Jesus want to walk how he walked, and this influences how he will interact with you. For example, if your man does something that hurts your feelings and you bring it to his attention, he'll acknowledge it, apologize, and make it right, as opposed to a quick, "Well, don't be so sensitive." He'll know he's not perfect and, while striving to do the right thing, will realize that life comes with making mistakes—and he will own up to it.

Men who love Jesus want to walk how he walked.

Have you ever noticed how disarming it can be when someone tells you they're sorry? Not to mention it's incredibly attractive. Almost instantly my defenses go down and I think, "Oh, you're just a human like me." If the guy I was dating were perfect all the time, I would feel an immense amount of pressure to live up to that and be perfect myself. My guess is that I'd fail on the first day. But he can be perfect for me—and that's the difference. Being perfect for me means that "I'm sorry" are words that have an entry in his personal dictionary.

In my most recent relationship, it seemed as though I was apologizing every other week for something. It wasn't because I was taking responsibility for something that wasn't mine to own; I genuinely needed to apologize. However, so did he. But he never did. In fact, not one time in our dating relationship did I hear anything remotely close to the words "I'm sorry" flow out of his mouth. That's not humility—that's pride. It should have been a red flag. In the future, I will wait for the man who is not afraid to admit when he is wrong.

You may be wondering, "Well, how do I recognize humility through a dating profile or through text messaging when I'm first getting to know him?" It can be normal to misinterpret texts when first getting to know someone, particularly with no context of that person's personality to filter the messages through. When it's clear that you're unsure of what he was trying to communicate and you text a clarifying question, is he quick to respond with, "I'm sorry, I meant [fill in the blank]?" Or, do you consistently get frustrated emoticons with short responses that cause you to regret you asked? Another clear sign of lack of humility, before I even decide to swipe in any direction, is if his entire profile is filled with shirtless mirror selfies captioned with his max bench press. Zero humility. Move on.

3. *Pursuit.* All the women were unanimous that one of the most attractive qualities in their boyfriends (now husbands) was that he pursued them. Not only did the men pursue the women while dating, but they also pursued the women after they were married. The idea of being pursued by a man is tossed around a lot in Christian circles.

From the time they are in high school, Christian girls are told to wait for the man who will pursue them.

Equal opportunity for genders and feminism have made this whole idea cloudy at times. In the way that God made the first move toward us in initiating a relationship, men want to do the same. If we let them. Even when we meet a guy on a dating app, he can still pursue us. This means he asks us on a date first (even if it's just a text), he decides on the location, and he picks the time. He doesn't leave it up to you; he puts in the forethought and then communicates that plan to you.

When you are pursued by a man, you don't have to wonder where you stand with him, or if he is interested in you. He will be direct and tell you. Most women told me that it was never a guessing game while dating. Multiple times they said that when their future husband asked them out, they all offered versions of, "I would like to date you because I'm interested in you, so I am going to keep asking you out because I want to keep getting to know you." As the relationships progressed, so did the clarity from the men. The men continued to be clear and direct with their intentions. The men communicated throughout the week, letting the women know they were thinking about them. While together, the men continued to pursue the women by asking intentional questions, and then following up with additional questions, letting the women know that there was a genuine interest beyond shallow one-word answers. While dating and once married, the men planned dates with her in mind. By taking initiative and putting forethought into how they'd spend their time together, it communicated to the woman that he valued time together by not allowing it to be an afterthought.

There was one guy I dated who did anything but pursue me. In fact, I'm not entirely sure I can use the word *date* because I never had clarity if that is what we were even doing. What I do know, however, is that I don't want to be someone's afterthought. I don't want to fish for answers, or have to deduce that he is interested in me based on vague texts or spontaneous interactions. The relationship worth waiting for will be void of either of those things.

Likewise, women, you also have a responsibility to be clear in your responses to his pursuit of you. Meet his intentions with equal directness. I believe that this honors what Jesus has commanded us to do when he says to love others like we love ourselves: when he is direct with you, you are direct back. If you like him, tell him. If you appreciate the gestures, communicate that to him. If he calls or texts you, respond to him. If you are no longer interested, be clear about that too. Don't leave him guessing.

4. *Chivalry.* It is incredibly honoring when men open the door for women. Or allow her to walk up the staircase first, wait so she's the first one out of the elevator, or carry her bag. It's especially kind when he pays on the first few dates. Does any of this mean that women cannot open the doors for themselves or hold a respectable job that allows them to afford their own meals? Absolutely not. But it does mean this is one way he can show you that he honors you. In return, when you allow a man to do these things for you, it's a way of showing him respect. Most couples I spoke with noted this in their relationship.

When a man tries to pay for your meal or open your door and you roll your eyes, shrug him off, or say, "No thanks, I can do it," it's a subtle way that you are disrespecting him. Disrespect may not be your intention, but men (good men) want to care for women, and they do this by providing for and protecting them. Men love to spend money on what they value. If he wants to spend money on you, he is communicating that he values you. (Side note: if he doesn't reach for the check, or agrees to going Dutch, he may be communicating that he is not interested.) Chivalrous men will say to you at the end of the night, "Text me when you get home so I know you made it home safely." They will walk you to your cars when it's dark, wait to be sure you made it in your house before driving away, and they will be sure that your car starts. That is what chivalry looks like, and it's worth waiting for.

Women, as a side note, most men commented that they loved that their wives were grateful—not entitled—while dating. It's one thing to allow men to do these things for us; it's another thing when we expect or even demand it. This is another way that you can honor God by treating the man the way you want to be treated. It doesn't mean that you pay or open the door, but it does mean that *if* you were to do those things, you would want someone to show appreciation to you. You may be internally grateful, but no verbal gratitude implies ingratitude. For me, it never gets old when a man opens my door or pays for my meal. I never expect it, but I feel so honored when he does it. I look him in the eye and tell him, "Thank you." And I mean it.

Some Things Never Change

Some of you are in relationships right now; maybe that list doesn't sound like you and your boyfriend. When you think about it, you know that he is not quite the man you thought you were waiting for. But you justify it away because anyone can change. After all, some-times he's the man you were waiting for—just not all the time. If you are thinking he *will change*, my caution to you is to be careful. You need to be comfortable with the fact that he *may never change*. Changed behavior once, anyone can do; real change is repeated behavior over time. When you date someone with an issue you have to ignore, you're settling. Don't do that.

I dated a guy who was such a gentleman when we were alone. He loved God and honored me, and our conversations were rich and intentional. He was respectful, kind, and considerate. But when we were out in public, it was a different story. He was still most of those things to me, but from a distance. The impression he gave to others when I was around was that I was a good friend at best, not someone he was interested in. Red flag! I learned this lesson the hard way: Who he is publicly is still who he is privately. He was dealing with some unresolved insecurities, which when we were alone seemed to be no big deal. But the way they manifested themselves publicly was that he wasn't sure I was good for his public image.

Wow. When I finally opened my eyes to the truth of the situation, it hurt. The right man won't be embarrassed by you—or me. In fact, it will be the exact opposite. He will be so proud of who you are that he will want everyone to know it. I have several great guy friends who

are currently in serious dating relationships. They are so proud of their girlfriends that it's all they can do to talk about something other than them. It's really sweet. The right men do those sorts of things.

Your Best Version

One last thing to look for in a relationship: If he doesn't bring out the best in you, he's not the best for you. The right man will make you want to be a better woman. He will push you to be the very best version of yourself. You become like the people you spend the most time with. That is especially true for the person you are dating. When you look at him, do you think to yourself, "I want to become the type of person he is"? Because whether you want to or not, you will become like him.

Isn't it true that we rise and fall to the level of expectations set on us? The same is true in dating. If we expect him to be a gentleman, he will be. Likewise, if men have experiences from some women as being easy, inappropriate, or rude, then men begin to expect that from all women. But if we expect their best selves and set the standards for value, priorities, and honor, they will step up. We can complain all we want about a lack of decent men out there, but are we expecting them to be decent? Are we interacting with them in such a way that communicates that's what we expect?

It's a cycle: when we expect and bring the best out of them, they expect and bring the best out of us, and around it goes. We are constantly teaching people to interact with us either in ways we like or in ways we don't like. If we want men to treat us well, then we need to set the standards up front. The right guy won't be offended by that. In fact, it will be attractive to him and he will reciprocate. The result is that we are helping the other person to be the best version of themselves.

You may be thinking, "But I'm not dating anyone right now. How exactly am I supposed to practice this stuff?" When I was in college, my roommates and I were discussing the topic of dating and marriage. We looked at one another and said, "While we are all single and living together, we are going to commit to putting the other person first, loving each other like God tells us to love, and practicing the hard conversations when the need comes up." We were nineteen and twenty at the time and didn't know a whole lot about—well, a lot of things. But we did know that most great things in life take commitment, intention, and time. So we decided we'd practice with each other, with the goal of preparing us better for the men we'd (hopefully) one day marry. This concept has stayed with me throughout my adult years. There is always an opportunity to get better at loving God and to get better at loving other people, which also helps you recognize the men who are committed to that same thing. You may not be in a dating relationship currently, but I guarantee there are plenty of other people in your life to cultivate relationships with while you wait.

When we involve dating apps, it's easy to hide behind the screen and have interactions that we wouldn't necessarily have if we were face-to-face. It's easy to justify those interactions as funny or entertaining, but remember, in the same way we are looking for that one relationship worth waiting for, men are too. I've been on dating apps, and so I know: sometimes the virtual interactions are anything other than right. But I believe the more we maintain a standard of decency regardless of the interaction on the other side, the more the interactions on the other side will rise to the occasion. Until eventually the ones we swipe will all become men worth waiting for.

Questions for Reflection

1. Have you ever watched a romantic comedy and held out hope that you'd be in a relationship like that? What about the relationship in the film attracted you? What about the relationship seemed unrealistic?
2. Practically speaking, what would it look like to implement Jesus's Golden Rule in your dating relationships?
3. Have you ever dated someone who didn't bring out the best version of you? What do you think it would look like to date someone who does bring out the best of you?
4. Are there additional qualities you've seen in great relationships that you hope to emulate?

--------------------[C H A P T E R   9]--------------------

Communication

Communicating means transmitting information, thoughts, or feelings so they are satisfactorily received or understood. In other words, it's one thing for you to provide information, but it's another thing for the person on the receiving end to comprehend the information in the same manner as you intended to deliver it. Both steps are involved.

The inherent challenges of communication remind me of the telephone game we used to play when we were kids. Everyone would sit in a circle. The first person whispered a sentence into the ear of the person to their right. That person whispered the phrase as they heard it into the person's ear to their right. The game continued until the last person in the circle had received the phrase. The game concluded with the last person saying the phrase out loud. Although the goal was to relay the message without alteration, part of the entertainment came from seeing the twisted nature of the original message once the last person repeated it out loud. I will never understand how the sentence: "The brown dog went outside to play with his owner who threw him a red ball" turned into: "The corn on the cob was outside on the ledge near a boomerang." But isn't that how communication works sometimes? What we say is not always what is heard, regardless of how clear we think we are.

This is especially true in relationships and their multiple layers of communication. The first involves the person actually providing the information. Are they being clear and direct and actually saying

What we say is
not always what is
heard, regardless
of how clear
we think we are.

what they mean? Or are they saying what they think the other person wants to hear? There's a difference. The second layer is even trickier. The person on the receiving end will filter what they are hearing through their own personality, their past, their current mood, and their experiences with the person communicating to them. Then add the emotions of both parties to the mix, and it puts added weight on the message being communicated. Wow, that's a lot! With all those things going on, it's a miracle we even communicate at all. Since there is definitely an art to communicating well, it's even more important that we get this art right in relationships. But that's the good news: It is possible to have great communication, even with the person you're dating.

I'm guessing some of you are like me. You've found yourself in situations with someone where you've said, "I didn't say that!" or "How did you get *that* out of what I was saying?" Or a sarcastic text you sent got totally misinterpreted on the receiving end, leaving you with multiple screens of back-and-forth explanations. Those are the worst. Modern-day reality presents us with multiple avenues for communication. The good news is that no one is without an excuse for not communicating. The bad news is there are multiple ways for us to misunderstand each other. Before the internet, we really only had two options: the telephone and face-to-face conversations. In addition to that, we now get to text, DM, snap, app message, and tweet. Just to name a few. I don't know; what could possibly go wrong with all those options (insert sarcasm)?

Dating apps add an interesting factor to the relationship equation. We want the men in our lives to "man up," so to speak, pick up the phone, and ask us out. We find ourselves wondering why he isn't bringing up that topic we were just texting about, when he seemed so adamant about it prior to sitting down face-to-face. On the other hand, the reason a date is even a possibility is because we've met him through an app on our phones, so our relationship began virtually. It can be difficult to backpedal and minimize virtual chat when we've already set the expectation that digital communication is acceptable. I'm not arguing that it's not. Trust me, there are plenty of times when

I'd rather text instead of call because of the sheer speed and effectiveness of communicating what I need—and getting a response. However, I think there is a time and place for it. Recognizing that time and place is a delicate balancing act. The goal is that you'll finish this chapter knowing how to discern when texting or speaking in person is more appropriate, and recognize the potential pitfalls of building a relationship exclusively online.

To Text or Not to Text

In a world where it feels quicker to communicate without ever picking up the phone or meeting in person, it's also become increasingly common to use these same popular forms of electronic communication to communicate things that never should have been put in writing in the first place.

What do I mean by that? Electronic communication is emotionless. No matter how many exclamation points, smiley faces, and boldface words you use, the message still falls flat on the reader's screen. All emotion read into your email is entirely up to the discretion of the recipient. What's even worse is that any ambiguity in your email will almost always be skewed toward the negative. As humans, we tend to default to worst-case scenarios.

How many of you have gotten together with your girlfriends, put on your detective hats, and tried to decode a text message from a guy? He used a winky face; what do you think that means? His punctuation included a period, not an exclamation point. Is that bad? Or he didn't use any punctuation. Do you think he's excited or just patronizing me? His reply just said, "Cool." Does that mean he wants to go or not? I'm not sure if he's interested; it took him two hours to reply. (You know we all live for those bubbled dots in our text box.)

The way we analyze and agonize over text messages is exhausting. It feels like it takes a PhD to decipher the meaning behind the words, and even then we sometimes get it wrong. I once had a guy text, "Why are you yelling at me? You used an exclamation point." My reply: "I'm not yelling, that's how girls text excitement or fun!" Him: "It's yelling." On and on we went, now texting about something completely irrelevant to the original content (talk about losing the point). You can imagine how annoyed we both got.

Ironically, digital communication has gotten even more ambiguous with the rise of emojis. Emojis are the new emotions. Why would you actually say what you are feeling when you can send a digital representation? One of my guy friends who is in his thirties recently told me that he had to figure out what all these emojis meant in text messaging. I wondered what his newfound love for emoji-speak was all about, but didn't put too much thought into it. Then he explained that he just began a new relationship with a girl in her twenties and she consistently sent texts of emojis instead of words. This was something he had not encountered when dating women from his own decade. As if deciphering the meaning behind the words wasn't hard enough, we now have to interpret the visual representation of an emotion through digitalized hand gestures, cartoon characters, landmarks, and other symbolic icons. I thought the digital age was supposed to simplify, not complicate! My guy friend felt as though he was trying to learn a new language just to date this girl. Emojis are fun, but I'm not sure they should be a replacement for words. At least, not when it involves content that matters.

Girls, remember this reality: Messages on a screen are open to interpretation, according to our mood—or the recipient's—at the time, current circumstances, and past experiences. The space that exists between texts can cause us or the other party to interpret, reinterpret, and misinterpret. Is that worth the risk when your relationship is on the line?

A former boss of mine gave me some of the best advice when it comes to appropriate and inappropriate use of digital communication. At the time of our conversation, society's common context was email, but I apply this rule to anything outside of verbal communication. *Electronic communication should be used for information and affirmation only. Everything outside of those parameters should be communicated in person.* In other words, if it isn't affirmative or informative, say it, don't text it. This applies to email, texting, DM, and anything else you can think of.

If it isn't affirmative or informative, say it, don't text it.

If you are communicating facts, dates, a time to meet, or anything of that nature, then by all means text away. If you have a quick word of praise or encouragement for a job well done, then again, text it. If you are running late, stuck in traffic, or need to change an appointment time, sending off a few words will do the trick. There is no ambiguity in any of those things.

However, if there is any hesitation on your part that what you are writing can be misinterpreted, then pick up the phone. If you have bad news to deliver or a topic that needs further conversation for clarity's sake, then pick up the phone. If you begin typing and your words are now overflowing onto the second screen, pick up the phone. I will be the first to admit that it's far easier to hide behind a screen to say the things that I shy away from when speaking the words in person. But for the sake of clarity and respect for the other person, I have chosen to think twice about what I put in writing.

Let's Talk

Relationships can be complicated enough. Let's not add to that with our methods of communication. There is a reason that certain topics should be left for face-to-face time (not to be confused with FaceTime). Instead, let important topics of conversation be a conversation—in person. It's not worth the risk to have things that are important be open to interpretation.

When our emotions are running high, it can feel easier to shoot off a text. The benefit of texting is that it affords us the opportunity to say things that we may not feel as comfortable saying in person. How many times have you tried to muster up the strength to bring up a point of tension with the guy you were dating—you even went over the talking points with your girlfriend beforehand—but when push came to shove, you defaulted to a text? Texting just seemed easier, didn't it? You could say what you wanted to say without the consequences of the reaction on his face. We've all done it. I certainly have. And men have done it to me.

But that's where we confuse ourselves. If we wouldn't say it in person, then we definitely shouldn't say it over text. If you find yourself texting commentary of a serious nature minutes after you just spent time with that person, let that serve as a warning to you that you're hiding behind a screen. It's not fair to the other person.

It takes two people to have a face-to-face conversation, though. I once had a guy refuse to have a conversation with me. We had had some pretty intense interactions of late, so I asked him if we could meet up and talk about it. He claimed to be too busy. He told me there was no way he was going to be able spare an hour for an in-person conversation because he just had too much going on. This cat-and-mouse game over text went on for well over a month. When we finally met in person—mind you, our in-person exchange totaled about fifteen minutes, because he just "had" to rush off to the next thing—I pressed him on why it took so long to have this conversation. His reply? That was his way of "protecting" the relationship, by giving us space and not talking about it. Yet, he would text me multiple screens on the subject matter. That is the most dysfunctional thing I've ever heard. Trust me, I recognized it as soon as it came out of his mouth. That was also the last conversation he and I ever had. If someone does that to you, don't fall for it. It's a sign of immaturity.

If someone tells you they are too busy to talk, but they're happy to text about it, I would suggest they are not being truthful. We all make time for the things that are most important to us, regardless of how busy we are. So, what he is communicating is that you are not important enough to make time for. In these instances, I would encourage you to place strong boundaries around your text interactions. Specifically, if he tries to engage in a tough topic over text, your reply should simply be: "I'm happy to talk about this in person." Trust me, I get it. It's hard to not engage in text exchanges of a personal nature when your mind is spinning with comebacks or additional points. We want to say it now and not have to wait.

Having hard conversations in person, and not over text, takes a certain level of vulnerability and trust. And vulnerability is a key to healthy, lasting relationships. When you commit to face-to-face conversations, you are also committing to growing in your trust in the person. Trust that you can be honest with him and he won't shy away, ignore you, or leave.

The truth is that learning to have healthy dialogue takes time and intention. We each have our own unique styles of communicating things because we have individual experiences that form the way we see the world, people, and relationships. Part of relationships is learning how to build a bridge between two divergent communication styles so that each person feels heard, understood, and valued—even if it means we don't always see eye to eye. With something that important, wouldn't you want to do that in person?

Emotional Relationships

While we're talking about hiding behind our words, I would be remiss if I didn't address emotional relationships as they relate to texting. Two people can emotionally date without ever physically dating. You rarely see each other in person, but you text. A lot. About everything. You share details of the day, relate exciting things that have happened, and ask each other advice. When friends notice that you are texting this person with increased frequency, what's your reply? "But we're just friends." Huh? If he is the person you want to text before anyone else, then he has become your primary emotional confidante, and, no, you are not "just friends." If you find your thoughts drifting toward him throughout the day, you may be in an emotional relationship. Do you think about all your other friends this much throughout the day? Probably not.

The reason this can be so dangerous is because you're cheating yourself out of a real relationship. When you are giving so much of your emotional attention over text to a guy who you are not even dating, you have created very little emotional capacity for the right guy to come into your life. Chances are you may not even notice him if he did come along. Don't give up your future to someone who won't even be in it.

Now you may be thinking, "But we've developed a real relationship. If you saw the content of our text exchanges, you'd understand." Believe me, I do understand because I've been there. Chances are you have developed some sort of emotional bond. When you find yourself in this place, I see one of two options. The first is he steps up his game and moves the relationship into real time. You spend actual time together in the evening or on the weekends. The second option is you cut it off. I can't speak for men, but women invest our hearts in relationships like these. That's why they are called *emotional* relationships. And if it continues for any considerable length of time without further commitment, it feels like a breakup for the girl when it finally does end. Which is a place you don't want to find yourself in—mourning the loss of a guy you never even dated. I encourage you to pay attention to the amount of emotional energy you are investing and to walk away when texting with him becomes the sole place where you are confiding in him.

Actions Still Speak Louder Than Words

Another danger of relationships that are primarily digital is that some people act very differently online than in person. Over text, it's too easy to build a persona and say what you think the other person wants to hear. A friend of mine recently told me that she was matched with a guy through Hinge. Within minutes of the connection, they exchanged phone numbers and began a seven-day text exchange. To her it was fun; and she felt as though they were building a relationship. Her best guess is they exchanged nearly a thousand texts throughout that week, every day, covering hundreds of topics. They texted about lighthearted topics and more serious ones. During their exchanges, he told her how beautiful she was and how much he liked her.

Eventually, on day seven, they arranged to meet that night for dinner. Driving to meet him, she felt like she was going to meet up with her boyfriend—the difference being that they'd never met in person. Excited, she walked in the door and found him, and they grabbed a table. Immediately she felt awkward and uncomfortable—and verbalized it. For seven days, they had built a false sense of intimacy through text messaging. Across the table, he didn't act like the guy she had been texting with every day.

I think of it the same way a great book leaves me disappointed when it is translated (poorly) onto the movie screen. I have a certain way of imagining the characters in my book, and when I see their portrayal in the theater, it doesn't always live up to my expectations. For seven days my friend had built a relationship in her mind based on assumptions and expectations, all of which were inferred through messages on her phone. But they didn't completely line up with reality. Now granted, this isn't entirely her fault. She could only form her opinion from what he had messaged to her. Regardless, that's the risk you take when texting with a stranger.

He had said that honoring God and respecting women were his top priorities; my friend had read all those things on her phone prior to this dinner. However, by dinner's end it was apparent he had been texting what he thought she wanted to hear. He pushed her physically that night, much further than she wanted to go, though not as far as it could have been. Granted, she gave in, but she left that night feeling disappointed and guilty. As a side note, if you have ever found yourself in this situation, don't beat yourself up for too long. There is grace. We learn from our mistakes, get up, and try again. This time, a little bit wiser.

 If his texts are telling you one thing but his actions are telling you something different, he may only be texting what you want to hear.

If his texts are telling you one thing but his actions are telling you something different, he may only be texting what you want to hear. It doesn't matter what he texts you, do not take his beliefs seriously until they show up in how he behaves. Why is this so important? The phone is where you can hide if you want. It acts as a screener. You put your best foot forward—but only on screen. You only type and send the best parts of yourself. You can play any role you want through a screen. You can say what the other person wants to hear, but it's only when you get in front of the other person that real life starts to play out. Is he as kind, gentle, and funny as he seemed when you were just texting? I don't know how many times I've had men text me things that didn't add up when we were in person. I would typically end up on my couch that night second-guessing myself, feeling completely confused. Then he would show up on my phone, text what I wanted to hear, and the cycle would start all over. Thankfully I got a clue and moved on, though not without heartache.

A Note About Sexting

Texts live forever. You can't take it back. Once you hit "send," you have no control over who sees it. Which brings me to sexting. To be clear, sexting is sending sexually explicit messages or photographs, typically via mobile phones. Don't do it. Ever. It's objectification. If he asks for a picture of your naked body, the extent of his interest is in your body, not you. If you comply, you are affirming that in him. I have heard too many stories where pictures of him or her ended up on the phones of "just their best friends." How many times have you heard of a couple breaking up and suddenly nude photos of one of them circulate through their entire social circle? It happens.

You may think this only applies to pictures. It doesn't. If your text exchanges cross the line from comfortable to uncomfortable for you, that is a serious red flag. You are under no obligation to reply. I had this happen to me. It was with a guy I was casually spending time with. We were just getting to know each other. We were in a text exchange late at night (red flag number one), and out of nowhere I saw a text that said, "Tell me what you'd want to do to me if we were together right now." I was shocked. I wasn't sure how to reply. In my pause, a few more texts came through my phone, a bit more explicit in nature. I was confused. Here was this man—who was sup- posedly a God-honoring man, I might add—sending me messages like this. I enjoyed spending time with him; he was someone I had a lot of respect for. But this? In the moment, his interest crossed over from me to using me to fulfill a late-night fantasy, probably fueled by loneliness. I think I replied, "I'm sorry, I can't do that." He pressed it a few more times over the next thirty or so minutes (via text of course), but eventually dropped it.

Looking back now, I should have been clearer with my standards, including the fact that texts of that nature are not appropriate. But I wasn't. That relationship had a short shelf life, and over time I found out that was his normal MO for interacting with girls through text. This from someone who reportedly loved God and even held positions of influence in the church. It just goes to show that sexting knows no boundaries and you'd be wise to stay far away from it. Regardless of who is sending it to you, it's never okay and you don't need to give in.

God and Our Conversations

Communication is important. God teaches us a great deal about it. After all, God himself is a communicator. He spoke creation into existence and thereafter used words to teach us about how to live well. One of the wisest men in the Old Testament, Solomon, told us that our tongues have the power of life and death (Prov. 18:21). Because you and I are made in the image of God, we also have power in our words: we can both destroy and encourage others with them. Whoever said that "sticks and stones may break my bones, but words will never hurt me" was mistaken. We know this to be true by the wounds from words (via text and in person) that still plague us today. In light of this, God cares about how we communicate, and it is especially important for us to communicate well in our relationships.

Here are three tips for communicating well that, if implemented, can go a long way.

1. *Speak words to build up, not tear down.* When Paul, the author of several New Testament letters, was giving instructions about daily life to the Ephesians, he made a point to tell them to only say what was helpful for building others up, speaking things that would be

beneficial to them (Eph. 4:29–30). Why? Because we, like the Ephesians, so often speak things that we perceive as beneficial to us, not
thinking about the effect they are going to have on the other person. When we are speaking to the guy we are dating, imagine if we
put ourselves in his shoes and felt the potential weight of our words
before they came out of our mouths. How much would that change
our word choices?

2. *Practice listening.* Another New Testament author, James, tells
us to be quick to listen, slow to speak, and slow to become angry
(James 1:19). It's interesting to me that James tells us to be slow to
speak within the context of anger. I have to think he knew how easy
it is to fire off careless words when emotions are running high. But
instead, when we listen first without merely just thinking of our next
statement, we begin to learn more about the other person's perspective. In relationships, this is one way that we can honor the other
person and value their thoughts and feelings. Imagine how that could
change or grow your relationships!

3. *Be honest.* While you may think that hiding your true feelings
is sparing the other person, in the long run not being truthful can
end up doing more harm than good. In the same breath that Paul
spoke to the Ephesians about words of encouragement, he also told
them to put off falsehood and to speak truthfully (Eph. 4:25). Not
being truthful to the person you are dating is called lying. We don't
typically think of it that harshly, but it is. Think about it this way:
If you are not being honest with him, are you really giving him the
opportunity to know the real you? If you don't tell him when he has
hurt your feelings or done something that made you feel special, then
he won't know. You can't expect him to know something that you've
never directly said.

Beginning a relationship with a guy through an app doesn't make
us exempt from healthy in-person communication. Practicing these
tips now, while dating, will go a long way in marriage.

Dreams Do Come True

I was talking with a girlfriend the other day. She had been married a month earlier to a respectful, kind-hearted, God-honoring man. But prior to meeting her Mr. Right, she had been on four dating apps and had connected with a handful of men. She wasn't entirely happy with the way her interactions with these guys had turned out. As she began new relationships, their interactions had become predominantly digital. She rationalized it as "that's just the way it is." Until she met her husband. Within the first few minutes of their connection, he texted, "May I call you?" It caught her off guard. Not because she didn't want him to but because it felt like a long-lost reality that might never resurface again. But it did. Or rather, he did.

From the very beginning of their relationship, they kept texting to an exchange of facts. He always arranged dates via a phone call, and as the relationship progressed he never got lazy or relaxed in how he communicated with her. She told me that, if anything, he became clearer and more direct in his verbal communication. If there was any sort of ambiguity in a text exchange, he quickly replied, "Let's talk about this tonight when we are in person."

The reason I like this example is because even though the two met on a dating app, the guy understood that certain topics are still best discussed in person. For my girlfriend, she had begun to wonder if any men understood the differences between online and in-person communicating. However, he wanted there to be no questions about his intentions or comments, so it was important that she heard his voice and could hear the tone, minimizing potential confusion around his intentions. Texting most certainly had its place in their relationship—and still does. But not with the things that are most important.

Isn't it a wonderful thing to know that respectful single men still exist, and that they have not lowered their personal standards of communication in a relationship due to cultural trends? I know I am always encouraged by stories like these. I hope you are too. Because the truth is that the man who respects you will also respect you in how he communicates with you. You don't need to settle for anything less. Setting your standards in communication will keep the right men coming back and keep the wrong men far away from you.

Dreams still come true.

Questions for Reflection

1. Describe a time when you got frustrated during a text conversation. What frustrated you? In hindsight, how could you have handled the conversation better?
2. Have you texted something that would have been better said in person? If so, what caused you to text it instead?
3. Which one tip from the "God and Our Conversations" section could you implement to develop better communication skills in your dating relationships?

Don't Waste Your Wait

Waiting is hard. It requires a certain level of patience and determination. I remember when someone offered me and a group of friends box seats to a Taylor Swift concert fourteen months before the show. Regardless of what you think about her and her decisions, most would agree she is a musical icon and puts on a good show. Besides, even if you're not a fan, it's likely you wouldn't pass up box seats to Taylor. I was ecstatic. *But how in the world was I going to wait fourteen months?* It felt like forever. Nevertheless, I persevered. When the day finally came, I—along with fifteen other adults over the age of thirty-five—loved every minute of it. I can confidently testify it was worth the wait, and then some. Should I find myself in the same situation again, I would wait those months all over again.

There are other things, however, where my ambition for putting in the wait wanes. Waiting for the job offer, acceptance letter, the invitation, or the second date. Or any date at all. You would think that dating apps would make waiting easier. Matches can be instantaneous, and yet it still feels like light-years of Taylor Swift–style waiting just to see if he'll swipe in the same direction. Despite the advances in technology, waiting is still waiting, and our smartphones haven't alleviated the pain we feel as we wait.

Several years ago, while I was living in Denver, the mother of all snowstorms came through during Christmas, shutting down the airport for three days. Did I say during Christmas? It was awful. Fortunately, I had the luxury of waiting it out in my own home. Others were not so lucky. Many were already at the airport when the storm hit, leaving them stranded. Being stuck overnight at the airport during Christmas is a different kind of awful.

A few friends and I were all in the same situation, needing to fly out for the holidays. We decided we'd all walk over to a mutually agreed-upon house, sit down in the den, and start making calls to the airline. None of us could get through to an agent. Instead, we each got a similar message saying, "Thank you for holding. Due to the volume of phone calls, your call will be answered in approximately three hours." In case you missed that, let me repeat myself: three hours. Who wants to sit on the phone for 180 minutes? Apparently those of us who were interested in going home for Christmas. We waited.

We were thrilled when one of us managed to get through to a real person thirty minutes sooner than promised. It's funny to think about now, but we all started to cheer when a human voice came on the line after only two and a half hours. It's all in the context. The agent agreed to let us go single file on the same call to accommodate our flight adjustments to go home. The good news? We each had our flights changed at no charge. The bad news? Thanks to Mother Nature, nothing would be leaving from Denver International Airport before Christmas.

More waiting. Disappointment began to settle over us like a lead-lined blanket. When you are single and twentysomething (like me at the time), the thought of being stuck alone for a major holiday can feel overwhelming. Particularly when your original plan was something different. I remember making phone calls to my parents telling them I wouldn't make it. I could barely choke the words out.

Then we got a different type of phone call. A generous friend from California called to say they would charter a private plane for us from the commuter airport up the street. If that airport cleared the takeoff, ten of us could board the plane. We had to be ready in three hours. The private plane would take us to Southern California, and then it'd be up to each of us to figure out how to get home from there. Done! We each raced home to pack our bags.

Another phone call. The plane was cleared, but they couldn't get fuel into the airport. No fuel, no takeoff. A seesaw of emotions wracked my psyche. I stopped packing my bag. I waited. The final call came through, confirming there was no fuel at this particular airport. But they had found an airport one hundred miles away with the necessary fuel, and the pilot believed the plane could make it. Once there, he'd be able to fill up. If we could get to the plane in thirty minutes, he'd go for it. This was our only window of time before a second wave of storms moved in. If we missed it, there would be no second chances. I don't know what I packed, and I didn't care because I was getting on that plane in thirty minutes. We all were.

I remember when the plane finally took off and the ten of us cheered as if we'd personally won the Super Bowl. We yelled, exchanged high fives, and then stared in amazement out the window as we ascended over the Rockies. The overwhelming feeling was—we got out. A few of us had tears running down our cheeks, mine included. Albeit short, the end of the waiting period never tasted so sweet. Often, isn't that how waiting goes? Not only are there periods of premature celebration, but the final outcome isn't always what we had in mind. But it still works out, and you realize it's all going to be okay. You're okay and the outcome never tasted so sweet.

This kind of seesawing emotions is commonplace while we wait for Mr. Right. The number of times I thought I'd met him and the equal number of times when it turned out to not be true. He was someone's Mr. Right—just not mine. I can still remember how extreme both the highs and lows felt while trying to get out of Denver. I was desperate for relief from the agonizing wait to the point that I did nothing other than stare at the clock, watching the seconds tick by, waiting for news of a departure . . . or not. I wasted time while I was waiting. As I think about that story now, it feels all too similar to how it can go while waiting for the relationship that will end in I do. Our emotions dictate our wait and we waste precious time. But what if you didn't have to waste time while you waited—for either a date, a second date, or the man you're going to marry? I believe we can learn to take control of our waiting instead of allowing our waiting to take control of us. Even though the ending may be different than you would have written, you just might be better for it when you get there.

On Hold

In our lifetime, we have to wait for thousands of different things: waiting for an oil change, waiting in line at the grocery store, waiting for someone to text back, or waiting until we've saved up enough money to buy a new car or our first home. Then there are some of our most anticipated waits: waiting to get engaged or married. Waiting is a fact of life, but how we wait is up to us. Sometimes waiting feels like a holding pattern. It can feel helpless. At least for me, anyway. I feel like I have no control over the waiting.

I've noticed that when I call certain companies, I now have the option to receive a callback instead of sitting on hold. That's brilliant. How many times have you tried to get through to someone, only to be put on hold? For me, I'll switch to speaker mode and multitask while waiting. The ultimate letdown, though, is when someone finally does answer the phone after twenty minutes, only to inform me that I'll be transferred to another department. Then, somewhere in the midst of that transfer, I'm disconnected. It's in those moments that whatever initial resolve I had to persevere through the holding pattern has now run its course. I'm not sure I can muster up the strength for a potential repeat performance. Or worse, you call again and someone does answer, and all your anger regarding the repeat call has diminished. But it's not a someone, it's a computer. It's a trick. Reenter anger. More waiting.

However, thanks to technological advances, now I can ask for a callback. I no longer need to stay within earshot of my phone on speaker mode. I can get a few other things taken care of and be on hold at the same time. It's genius. Occasionally I'll get so caught up in whatever else I'm doing that the callback will actually startle me, and it can take a second to process who's calling.

When it comes to dating and marriage, I've repeatedly seen girls live their lives on hold. Recently I talked with a late-twentysomething girl about her next car purchase. She drove a smaller vehicle but was interested in getting something larger, possibly an SUV. She commented, "Even though I want an SUV, I don't want to buy it, because what if my husband has one?" I thought, *What?* She wasn't dating anyone at the time. This girl was making decisions, or not making decisions, based on someone who didn't even exist.

I remember when I finally decided to buy my first house. Growing up, little girls typically don't imagine that their adult story will involve purchasing their first home without a husband. Most of my single girlfriends are financially independent homeowners, and yet we've all had to work through the process of crossing this milestone solo. I'm not sure if society has subconsciously convinced us that women don't buy houses alone, or if somewhere along the way we've taught that to ourselves. Regardless, it's not the preference of most single women I know. And yet, we've all done it.

For me, I found myself getting jealous that my married homeowner friends could paint the walls in their house whatever color they wanted. I know, it's weird, but that was the tipping point for me. I had a choice. I could sit, wait, hope, and pray that I'd get married so that I could buy a house, or I could buy a house. Side note: Marriage does not equal homeownership, by the way. It's interesting that I and many others correlate the two. I decided that since I was financially secure, had made wise decisions, and had the current resources, I would buy a house. Not only did I do it, it represented one of the better decisions I've made in my adult life. There is nothing in me that feels "less than" because I made this purchase alone. Nor do I regret it. Do you want to know what the best part is? The walls in my house are whatever color I want!

Don't live your life out of a holding pattern.

I had to get to the point where I had to decide: Do I want to live my life out of a holding pattern or not? You need to make the same decision. There may be areas of your life where you are living out of a holding pattern and you don't even realize it. How do you know? If you've ever had this thought when making a decision of any kind: "But what if I get married?" That's an indicator that you may be making decisions based on a future potential rather than a current reality. Don't live your life out of a holding pattern.

Of course, there are some cases where that's okay to do. For example, if you are in a serious relationship, and you've mutually agreed that things are moving in the same positive direction, I can understand asking this question when it comes to renewing your lease, switching your health insurance, getting a puppy, or deciding on whether or not to take that job offer out of state. But if you are completely single with no immediate prospects in sight, I would argue this is not one of those times to ask yourself that question. The number one reason: there are no guarantees of marriage. Unfortunately, God did not say, "Let us create male and female in our image, and I promise that each one of them will be joined together in matrimony." I would have appreciated if that line was included in the first chapter of Genesis. But it wasn't.

 No thing or person can carry the full weight of our hope except God.

My friend Jeff said it best: when you live out of a holding pattern, "what you're waiting on becomes what you're hoping in."[14] That's a dangerous place to be. The reason it's so dangerous is because no thing or person can carry the full weight of our hope except God. No thing and no person can carry that weight. People were never designed to anyway. When we attempt to put our hope in people, circumstances, or things, we are setting ourselves up for disappointment and disillusionment. Why? Well, let's say all your hope is in a new job and you get it. But then you're fired. Or the company has cutbacks and you're a casualty. Or you climb the corporate ladder as high as you can go, and then what? What happens to your hope then? You need to find another outlet for it.

The same is true for marriage. God created us for intimate union with one another, and if you're reading this book, then you most likely have a desire for marriage. Me too. Despite that, our hope cannot be in marriage, because when it is and we're not married, it will unintentionally prevent us from living life fully. We won't accomplish the goals we want to accomplish—or we may not set goals at all. We may not pursue our dreams and instead settle for second or third best because it's easy and right in front of us. Then we'll think that once we're married, we'll chase after what we really want—in our profession, where we travel, or our athletic desires. All of this lends itself to putting our hope in marriage. That's a lot of pressure! Mainly because marriage isn't meant to be a solution, and if you're viewing it as such, you may be setting yourself up for disappointment and disillusionment.

I can't believe I'm going to admit this, but when I was eighteen years old, I bought myself my first Bible. That's not the embarrassing part, by the way. The store clerk asked me if I wanted my name engraved on the front. I had to go home and think about it. What if I got married and the wrong last name was forever imprinted on my Bible? I wrestled with that decision for weeks before finally making a decision. I thought to myself, *It's okay. When I'm married, I'll just get my new name engraved just above my maiden name.* That was twenty years ago. Had I made a decision out of a holding pattern, I would have been carrying around a nameless Bible for twenty years. Every now and then, my Bible cover will catch my eye, and my engraved name makes me laugh to myself. It's a subtle reminder to not live life out of a holding pattern.

Abraham and Sarah

God has some surprising things to say in the Bible about how to wait well. Abraham and Sarah were no strangers to waiting. It's easy to dismiss some of the life experiences of people in the Old Testament because their lives seem unrelatable to us in the twenty-first century. After all, they didn't live during a time of cars, electricity, telephones, or microwaves. On the other hand, most of our grandparents grew up in a world without color TV, smartphones, and the internet, and yet we don't dismiss their personal life experiences. Abraham and Sarah may have a lived a few thousand years before us, but their thoughts and feelings are no different from ours. Regardless of time period, all humans have the capacity for love, joy, hurt, and disappointment.

To catch us up to speed, when God first created the world, including man and woman, he made everything good (Gen. 1:31). But per usual, humankind made a mess of things and sin entered the world. God decided he was going to start over. The great flood wiped out almost everyone, except Noah and his immediate family. God then chose Abraham and Sarah to start generations of peoples who would bless the nations. But only after a looooooong wait.

Waiting wears us down. Abraham and Sarah felt that. God told Abraham to leave everything behind and go to a new land where God would make his descendants as numerous as the stars in the sky (Gen. 12:1–3 and 15:5). Mind you, Abraham had no children at the time. God promised to redeem all humankind, that the very line of Jesus would come through Abraham, and it was all going to start with Abraham and his wife. That's quite the promise. But God always makes good on his promises. Yet years went by and Abraham and Sarah were still childless.

Fair or unfair, people in Abraham and Sarah's culture stigmatized childless couples, kind of like Christian culture has associated a stigma with being single. This is a generalization, of course, but my guess is that you've all felt the weight behind the words: "I just don't understand why you're still single." I've heard this from well-meaning friends, family, and strangers alike. As if we didn't feel the weight enough, there is an underlying thought that you've somehow arrived once you're married. Arrived at what, I wonder? Double the car insurance? However, I can imagine that Abraham and Sarah felt a similar pressure. Except in their case the pressure was to have a baby. They lived in an era where children were a mark of the favor of God. But Abraham and Sarah had none. What must that have felt like? Disappointing? Disillusioning? Embarrassing, perhaps.

God came to Abraham again in a vision. You can hear the hurt in Abraham's voice when he replies, "Sovereign LORD, what can you give me since I remain childless? . . . You have given me no children; so a servant in my household will be my heir" (Gen. 15:2–3). Abraham had been waiting for God to make good on his promise, but still—nothing.

There are times when I've been waiting on God and have begun to lose hope. For me, job transitions have been some of my harder seasons of waiting. Particularly in my twenties, it was job rejection after job rejection. Dating relationships are certainly at the top of my list too. Waiting for the perfect guy while the seventeenth invite comes in, asking me to be a bridesmaid in a friend's wedding. Now, I know you know how this one feels. *Did God really mean that his plans for me were good? What good could God possibly give me?* I doubted. Maybe you've also experienced that. In his waiting, Abraham got impatient too. Yet we're told in the story that God reminded Abraham once again that he would have descendants too numerous to count (Gen. 15:5). Abraham believed God again. His faith was restored and I have to think this renewed Abraham's perseverance. He kept waiting.

One year. Two years. Lots of years. No baby. Some of you are familiar with that kind of waiting. When will it end? Will it end? God is clearly doing nothing. Sarah decided to take matters into her own hands. Abraham and Sarah had an Egyptian maid named Hagar, and since God had not come through on his promise, this couple decided to come through on their own. Sarah told Abraham to sleep with her maid, and that was how they would build a family. Abraham agreed, and Hagar gave birth to a son, Ishmael. However, this was not God's answer. Instead of being happy, the plan backfired. Furious, Sarah blamed Abraham for their servant bearing a child while she did not (Gen. 16:5). Now what?

This is the danger in waiting. Is it okay to feel as though God has forgotten about us? Or okay to feel that God changed his mind about promises that he made? Absolutely. Those are your feelings and you have every right to them. The danger lies when we begin to act on those feelings as if they are true. That was what Abraham and Sarah did. They doubted God's promises, convinced themselves that they were right, and acted on their own. They were tired of waiting, so they made their own way.

But here's the truth: God had not forgotten about them. Some of you need to hear that too: God has not forgotten about you. He doesn't forget. He can't. God is still at work, even in the waiting.

Fifteen years went by and God spoke to Abraham again. God told Abraham that at one hundred years old, he would father a son and his name was to be Isaac (Gen. 17:17–19). After Hagar had a son, fifteen more years passed before God spoke again. But this was the year God's promise would come to fruition in Abraham's life. Abraham and Sarah would have a son. Isaac continued the lineage that would eventually bring forth the child, Jesus, the Savior of the world. Although promised so many years prior, the promise most certainly did not come according to Abraham and Sarah's timeline. And what about the promise that Abraham's descendant would be as numerous as the stars in the sky? That happened, but Abraham never lived to see it (Heb. 11:11–12).

Becoming You

God had not forgotten about Abraham and Sarah. He was in the process of preparing them. During seasons of waiting for both you and me, God is in the process of preparing us too. We are not doing anybody any favors by living our lives on hold or by trying to take matters into our own hands. Too many single women I've known have tried to make their own path to God's plan when they got frustrated or lost hope with their nonexistent dating life. When that guy you like has yet to show interest, you figure out his regular traffic pattern and then show up "by chance." This looks like being on the sidewalk when he comes out of work, sitting in his section at church on Sunday during the hour he attends, or seeing a Facebook invite he responded yes to and showing up—even though you were not invited and don't even know anyone else who is going. To a few of you, these examples might seem extreme. To the rest of you, you know you've done this and more! This is what we do as women when we

feel hopeless: we want to take matters into our own hands and make him notice us.

I am not trying to dissuade you against giving hints to the guy you're interested in. That's normal. Of course it's okay to comment on his pictures when you've been matched on an app, or give him a smile if you pass him in person, or pay him an intentional compliment with a hand on his shoulder. Sometimes guys need to be encouraged that if they ask you out, you'll reciprocate with the same enthusiasm. But stalking the guy and showing up to go for an early morning walk in his neighborhood when you know he goes running every day at six *and* you live ten miles away is excessive. And weird. Don't do that.

Trust me, I get it. There are plenty of times where I feel like I'm living life on hold and am desperate to fix whatever "this" is. But God has plenty for you and me to do. Why? Because he doesn't want us to waste our wait. God was doing a work of preparation in Abraham and Sarah's life, and he does the same in us. There is a verse in the book of Ephesians that I come back to time and time again: "For we are God's handiwork, created in Christ Jesus to do good works, which God prepared in advance for us to do" (Eph. 2:10). Whether in a season of waiting or not, God always has a purpose and a plan for our lives.

Doing nothing has never been a part of the plan. Some Bible translations take the word *handiwork* to mean *workmanship* or *masterpiece*. The original meaning is "a thing that has been made."[15] In other words, God made you. He brought you into existence, creating you with a purpose in mind. You were not an accident, and your life is not some cruel joke. Instead, you were a great idea. A masterpiece. You were created on purpose for a purpose. A purpose that does not involve doing nothing. Waiting is not passive. Not when you understand you have work to do.

In moments when I feel like God has forgotten about me, I look back to the times when he tangibly reminded me that he had not. I have a very dear friend who, in an intense season of waiting, looked at me with tearstained eyes and said, "Kristin, God has been too faithful to me in the past for him not to be in the future." She's right. As unpredictable as God can feel at times, you can depend on his faithfulness. When our current reality causes us to doubt that God is really active in our lives, sometimes the only thing we can do is look to past markers of faithfulness to give us the hope we need to trust God with our future. It's interesting, but for me household issues can set me off and catapult me down the "woe is me, why am I still single, and does God care?" path. Particularly when something breaks or when I need to transport something heavy. Yet, I can look back and see the times when friends have stepped in who happened to know how to rewire my light switch. Or when the ones who were available had the bigger car and the man power to help me get that new TV or couch downstairs. God provides—even when it looks different than I imagined. God still shows up through people and reminds me that he sees me. The same was true for Abraham and Sarah: God's predictability doesn't always look like what we imagine.

Whether in a season of waiting or not, the Great Commandment still stands: love God and love people (Matt. 22:37–39). As we go through each twenty-four-hour day, we still have a responsibility to know God more, to love the people we come in contact with, and to be good stewards of this life that we have been given. I'm guessing that a lot of you are also like me in that you have big dreams for your life. God designed you like that. You have every reason to run hard after those dreams and to grow more and more into the person God created you to be. There is no other person who has your life experiences, your DNA, your skills, or your personality. You are the only one who can play the part of you. Don't waste that because you're waiting to get married. Life doesn't begin when you have a husband. Life began the day you were born. Everything else is extra. With that being said, what are you waiting for?

For me, I live my life without the idea of marriage even in the equation. It's not that I've given up, because I haven't, but a husband or boyfriend doesn't even factor into decisions that I make about my life. Why? Because that is not my current reality, so that means there is no need to consider someone who doesn't even exist in my present-day decisions. Instead of thinking that I'll travel a lot once I'm married, I've made the decision to see the world now—with friends. When I was in my early twenties, I used to believe that I didn't need to worry about saving for retirement because I assumed that I'd get married and those would be things my husband would take care of for both of us. However, there are no guarantees of marriage, and even if you do get married, there are no guarantees that he will be financially savvy. So I've been saving for my own retirement.

If you have career ambitions, then go for them now. If you want to go back to school for another degree, then do it now. If you want to move to another state, attend another church, take up a new hobby, or find a new social circle—what are you waiting for? Do it now. In my experience, I've found that God wants to know if I'm willing to say yes—to new things, to him, to trusting him in the process. And when I move forward, I've found that I learn to trust God in ways I hadn't before. I discover how much he is faithful in the details of something new, in the same way he was faithful in the old ways. I also learn that my life didn't fall apart because I decided to pursue my dreams or goals solo instead of waiting. In fact, it's been the opposite. I've made new friends, had more experiences, and gained an increased sense of self-confidence in what I'm capable of doing. Besides, if all you're doing is waiting until you get married, once you are married, then you'll just need to find something else to wait for. That doesn't sound like much fun.

The truth with waiting is that it's so easy to waste. It's easy to fall into the trap that the end result of whatever we're waiting for is the goal. But it's not. More times than not, the process of waiting, and what you do (or don't do) during that time is most important. Because the bottom line is this: you will never ever get that time back. So why not choose to do something with that time now while you still have it?

Or wait. And waste it all.

But don't do that. Don't waste the wait. It's not worth it. God works, even in the waiting.

Questions for Reflection

1. Can you relate to living your life in a holding pattern? Describe a decision or situation you put off in the past. What would it have looked like not to waste the wait?

2. How does it make you feel that God still has a purpose for your life during seasons where you feel like you are waiting? Do you find this difficult to believe? Why or why not?

3. What is one thing you can act on that you've put on hold?

Conclusion

I attended a wedding last month. The bride and groom were one of those couples who had a multiyear break in between seasons of dating. As the groom recited his vows to his bride, he said something like, "When you ended things with me five years ago, you looked at me and said I was not the man you needed me to be. And here we are five years later. Thank you for waiting for me to become that man for you now."

Don't ever be afraid to set standards for yourself. The right man will do the right thing, and if he doesn't, then he isn't the right man. If I've learned nothing else, it's that the wrong thing at the right time is still the wrong thing. Wait for the right thing. You deserve it. And remember: you will accept what you think you deserve. My job is to remind you that you only deserve the best. God's best. Don't settle for anything other than that.

Finding the right thing can feel impossible when dating apps have opened up so many options we didn't previously have. One would think options would be a good thing. But imagine walking up to your favorite ice cream counter. Instead of their regular six flavors, the shop decided to put every flavor they'd ever created on the menu. When you approach the counter to place your order, you now have forty-five flavors to choose from. The increased options have made your decision exponentially more complicated, not simpler. What if you choose the wrong one? Will you regret it? What if you want two flavors? What if the person next to you seems to be enjoying their flavor more than you?

Sometimes too many options can lead to indecision. Do you try something new even though it's not something you'd typically like? It's still new, so why not? Or do you stick with what you know you like—what works for you? What will you decide? Or do you not make a decision and simply walk away?

This is similar to how dating apps have changed the dating landscape. People approach dating like they approach too many flavors of ice cream. But it doesn't have to be like that. When you know what works best for you in a relationship and predecide to stick to your standards, you don't need to get sidetracked by a multiplicity of options. More options than you expected doesn't mean that you need to second-guess yourself or settle for something you're not interested in. You know what's best for you: honoring God with your own behavior, respecting yourself, and waiting for a guy who won't treat you like an option but makes you his priority. Stick with that and you'll be just fine.

Happily ever after is possible, and it's okay that it probably won't look like you imagined. My hope for you is that it's better. And when that happens, let me know!

Notes

1. Alexa Lyons, "Why Dating Apps Are Actually Great for Real Relationships," *Thrillist*, February 4, 2016, https://www.thrillist .com/sex-dating/nation/why-dating-apps-are-great-for-real -relationships.
2. "Olympics of Dating: Tinder Says Usage Is Skyrocketing in Rio," CBS News, August 9, 2016, http://www.cbsnews.com/news/the -olympics-of-dating-tinder-says-usage-is-skyrocketing-in-rio/.
3. Drew Harwell, "Online Dating's Age Wars: Inside Tinder and eHarmony's Fight for Our Love Lives," *The Washington Post*, April 6, 2015, https://www.washingtonpost.com/news/business/wp /2015/04/06/online-datings-age-wars-inside-tinder-and-ehar monys-fight-for-our-love-lives/?utm_term=.51a340582f43.
4. Andy Stanley, "#NoFilter" (sermon, Buckhead Church, Atlanta, GA, June 21, 2016).
5. "Dictionary.com's 2015 Word of the Year: Identity," Dictionary .com, accessed January 29, 2018, http://blog.dictionary.com /identity/.
6. Tania Lombrozo, "The Structure and Function of Explana-tions," *Trends in Cognitive Sciences* 10, no. 10 (October 2006): 464–70, https://doi.org/10.1016/j.tics.2006.08.004.
7. Meredith Faubel Nyberg, "Children in the New Testament, Graeco-Roman Context," in *The Lexham Bible Dictionary*, ed. John D. Barry et al. (Bellingham, WA: Lexham Press, 2016), n.p. See also N. S. Gill, "Roman Exposure of Infants," ThoughtCo., June 8, 2017, https://www.thoughtco.com/roman -exposure-of-infants-118370.

8. "Meet the New Hinge," *Medium*, September 27, 2016, https://medium.com/@Hinge/in-november-2015-a-team-of-20-decided-to-take-a-successful-mainstream-product-rebuild-it-from-the-a72f9155c6eb.

9. "Dating Apocalypse," TheDatingApocalypse.com, accessed January 29, 2018, https://thedatingapocalypse.com/stats/. The research findings are from surveys of 280 legacy Hinge users conducted in August 2016.

10. Andy Stanley, "#NoFilter" (sermon, Buckhead Church, Atlanta, GA, June 21, 2016).

11. Gerald Fadayomi, "The Great Escape" (sermon, Buckhead Church, Atlanta, GA, February 5, 2017).

12. Andy Stanley, "Session 9" (presentation, Catalyst Conference, Atlanta, GA, October 7, 2016).

13. Andy Stanley, "One-Another One Another" (sermon, North Point Community Church, Alpharetta, GA, August 3, 2013).

14. Jeff Henderson, "On Hold: Waiting On God Knows What" (sermon, Gwinnett Church, Sugar Hill, GA, February 18, 2017).

15. James Strong, "Poiéma," *The New Strong's Concise Dictionary of the Words in the Greek Testament and the Hebrew Bible* (Bellingham, WA: Logos Bible Software, 2009).

About the Author

Kristin Fry is a speaker, writer, and pastor, with nearly twenty years of ministry experience with twentysomethings. She was a staff member at North Point Ministries for seven years in Atlanta, Georgia. Currently she serves as a consultant and speaker. Kristin is passionate about encouraging women to dream big, take risks, and live the life they want.

Kristin has done postgraduate work at Dallas Theological Seminary and holds a master's degree in theological and biblical studies from Talbot School of Theology. Born and raised in California, she now makes her home in Atlanta.

Kristin would love to hear from you. You can follow her blog, contact her for speaking opportunities, or connect with her at KristinFry.com.